COOKING FOR HAPPINESS

Born in Ansbach, a small town in Bavaria, Kornelia Santoro worked as a journalist for a decade in Regensburg.

She met her Italian husband while riding an Enfield Bullet through India. They settled in Goa. After the birth of her son, Kornelia started writing cookbooks. She loves to experiment in the kitchen and explore the human relationship with food in a profound way. Her first two cookbooks, *Kornelia's Kitchen: Mediterranean Cooking for India* and *Kornelia's Kitchen 2: Cooking for Allergies*, have both won the Gourmand World Cookbook Awards. She also writes for media in India and Europe. She believes we are what we eat and happiness is a moment of bliss.

COOKING
FOR
HAPPINESS

KORNELIA SANTORO

HarperCollins *Publishers* India

First published in India in 2016 by
HarperCollins *Publishers* India

P-ISBN: 978-93-5029-765-0
E-ISBN: 978-93-5029-766-7

2 4 6 8 10 9 7 5 3 1

HarperCollins *Publishers*
A-75, Sector 57, Noida, Uttar Pradesh 201301, India
1 London Bridge Street, London, SE1 9GF, United Kingdom
Hazelton Lanes, 55 Avenue Road, Suite 2900, Toronto, Ontario M5R 3L2
and 1995 Markham Road, Scarborough, Ontario M1B 5M8, Canada
25 Ryde Road, Pymble, Sydney, NSW 2073, Australia
195 Broadway, New York, NY 10007, USA

Typeset in 10.5/14.5 Sabon by
R. Ajith Kumar

Printed and bound at
Thomson Press (India) Ltd

Dedicated to
Alberto, Valentino, Maria, Anneliese
And to you

CONTENTS

Preface   xiii

PART 1: NOURISH YOUR BRAIN

1. VITAMIN BOMBS   3
   ❦ Tabbouleh   5
   ❦ Rucola/Rocket/Arugula Salad   8
   ❦ Guacamole   11
   ❦ Cabbage and Carrot Salad   13
   ❦ Spinach and Mushroom Salad   16
   ❦ Stir-fried Broccoli   19
   ❦ Brussels Sprouts in Garlic Butter   23
   ❦ Gazpacho   26
   ❦ Pumpkin Soup   28
   ❦ Vegetables from the Griddle   31
   ❦ Chicken Liver Pâté   33
   ❦ Simple Granita or Sorbet   35
   ❦ Fruit Salad   37

2. BUILDING BLOCKS FOR THE BRAIN   40
    ♥ Roasted Chicken   42
    ♥ Chicken-Pesto Rolls   45
    ♥ Surprise Burgers   47
    ♥ Rocket Burgers   50
    ♥ Chicken-Carrot Cake   53
    ♥ Meat Loaf   55
    ♥ Rainbow Frittata   58
    ♥ French-style Omelette   60
    ♥ Russian Eggs   63
    ♥ Quinoa Spinach-Mushroom Pie   64
    ♥ Whole Wheat Pasta with Walnut Sauce   67
    ♥ Mexican Beans and Brown Rice   69

3. OMEGA-3 SOURCES   72
    ♥ Fish Soup   74
    ♥ Fish with Beurre Blanc   77
    ♥ Fish in Cartoccio   80
    ♥ Jumbo Crabs Asian Style   84
    ♥ Mussels Alla Marinara   87
    ♥ Oats and Tuna Burgers   90
    ♥ Ceviche   93
    ♥ Colourful Seafood Risotto   95
    ♥ Garlic Prawns with Brown Rice   99
    ♥ Tuna Pâté   101

4. HAPPY BELLY, HAPPY MIND   104
    ♥ Gigantes   107
    ♥ Indianized Fasolada   110
    ♥ Chickpea Soup   113
    ♥ Wheat Berries Risotto Style   115
    ♥ Mini Burgers   117
    ♥ Falafel   120

❦ Spicy Red Beans Salad 123
❦ Fierce Lentil Salad 125
❦ Hummus 128
❦ Bread Rolls 132
❦ Crackers with Salsa Dip 135
❦ Bran Muffins 138
❦ Chocolate-Chip Cookies 141
❦ Apple Pie 144
❦ Carrot Cake 146

PART 2: COMFORT FOOD 151

5. SAVOURY SUCCULENCE 153
❦ Pasta with Bacon and Cream 156
❦ Lasagne 158
❦ Zwiebelkuchen 161
❦ Homemade Pizza 165
❦ Ultimate Fried Potatoes 168
❦ Mashed Potatoes 170
❦ Crispy Chicken Drumsticks 173
❦ Chicken Soup 175
❦ Tzatziki 178
❦ Goan Prawn Curry 181
❦ Dal Makhani with Chapatis 184
❦ Thai Coconut Curry 188
❦ Thai Curry Pastes 190

6. SWEET MOMENTS OF BLISS 194
❦ Rice Pudding 196
❦ Bread Pudding 199
❦ Potato Latkes with Apple Sauce 201
❦ Creamy Cheesecake 204
❦ Key Lime Pie 208

   🍴 Delicious Spirals   212
   🍴 Profiteroles   215
   🍴 Coconut Triangles   218
   🍴 Apple Crumble   221
   🍴 Vegetarian Panna Cotta   224
   🍴 Crème Brûlée   226
   🍴 Qubani ka Meetha   228

7. THE CHOCOLATE HEAVEN   231
   🍴 Sachertorte   234
   🍴 Brownies   237
   🍴 Red Wine Cake   240
   🍴 Chocolate Cake   243
   🍴 Muffins   246
   🍴 Molten Lava Cake   249
   🍴 Chocolate Mousse   251
   🍴 Chocolate Cookies   254
   🍴 Truffles   256

8. KITCHEN MUST-HAVES   262
   🍴 Garlic Butter   264
   🍴 Onion Jam   266
   🍴 Chicken Stock   269
   🍴 Be Your Own Dairy Queen   272
   🍴 Pure Aroma   275
   🍴 Sweet Sauces   277
   🍴 Caramel Sauce   280
   🍴 Rum Raisins and Other Fruits in Alcohol   283

PART 3: STRESS-FREE DINNER PARTIES   287

9. ORGANIZATION IS KEY   289
   🍴 Dinner Party with Chicken   290

Dinner Party with Seafood   295
Vegetarian Dinner Party   300

Appendix: Measuring Ingredients with Tables   307
Bibliography   310
Acknowledgements   318

PREFACE

A few years ago, I considered writing a book about cooking for happiness. I wanted to tackle the subject from two fronts: nourishment for the brain and comfort food. This seemed like a rather manageable task. Sweet innocence!

Soon I discovered what a complex subject I had chosen. Scientists may have discovered quite a bit about the workings of our brain but many answers still elude them. The question of how food influences mood is quite a new one. Scientists started to investigate the subject seriously around twenty years ago. New discoveries have been published constantly.

I spent an entire year just reading everything I could find about the subject. I have written this book from a layperson's point of view and have recorded my own experiences, and backed them up with scientific facts for my readers.

I believe that simple pleasures can make us happy, so I have included the best comfort foods I have experienced in my life. The sheer delight of devouring them should not be underestimated – equally important is to eat food that supports the proper function of your brain and body. When you prepare them in your own kitchen, you avoid the pitfalls of processed foods, a big plus in my books. There is nothing wrong with a little cream and butter, and a lot of bacon, and chocolate!

Wishing you happy cooking, always!

PART 1

NOURISH YOUR BRAIN

'A sound mind in a healthy body'

JUVENAL, ROMAN POET

CHAPTER 1

VITAMIN BOMBS

Happiness is a moment of bliss because feelings never last. They are fleeting experiences by nature, but moments of bliss can be nurtured into appearing frequently. One major requirement for feeling fine is to have a nourished brain. You cannot expect your body and your mind to work well when your diet lacks essential nutrients and minerals. Vitamins play a key role in our well-being. Our bodies need them for many chemical processes, one of them being the synthesis of neurotransmitters in our brain. Lack of chemical function for neurotransmitters can cause depression and many other mental disorders.

Hence I start this book and my recipes by introducing 'Vitamin Bombs'. After eating one of the following dishes, try to discover the subtle feeling of wholeness that a healthy meal delivers. It may take a little while before you notice any change. Improving your mood with food takes time and patience but it is rewarding and safer than taking pills – although medication can help free you from the grip of depression.

Vitamins were discovered thanks to various diseases. The first illness recognized as nutritional deficiency was scurvy. While sailing for months, sailors developed weakness and blood spots, and lost their teeth. After reaching land and eating fresh fruits, they recovered. In 1617, the British physician John Woodall cured scurvy with lemon juice and persuaded the East India Company to provide lemon juice for sailors.

The term 'vitamin' was coined during the research on beriberi. Casimir Funk, a Polish biochemist in London, claimed he had found the missing nutrient responsible for beriberi. In 1912, he called it vital amines because he thought mistakenly, that it belonged to amines, the building blocks of proteins. A few years later his mistake was discovered, but a name was needed, so the term vitamin was born.

The puzzle of each vitamin was solved through the work of many scientists over many years. However, our understanding of vitamins continues to evolve and scientists keep discovering phytonutrients. Phytonutrients, or phytochemicals, are substances that help plants grow and flourish. They are active substances in the pigments of plant skins – literally the colours of nature.

HAPPY BY CHOICE

I have decided to be happy. It took me more than fifty years to reach this point – either I am a slow starter or maybe I am just more confused than others. I needed all these years to understand that happiness is not a mystical state that happens just so.

I am not a person who manages to be cheerful no matter what. I envy these fortunate characters – sometimes with the suspicion that they might be putting on an act and masking their feelings. Depression, gloom and suicidal desperation are states of mind I know well. During adolescence, I experienced the mental disease anorexia nervosa. My obsession with food started at that time, but I was only concerned with calories, carbohydrates and fats. Luckily, after a few years, my body regulated itself.

When I fell in love for the first time, I was happy. I spent three weeks in paradise, mostly naked, on a Greek beach. The paradise did not last when I joined my love in his home country. But I got to know Greek cuisine and I managed to keep a great figure without following any special diet.

In Greece, I discovered my love for salad. On most days we only had the typical Greek salad for lunch: tomatoes, cucumbers, black olives and red onion slices, topped with a slab of feta cheese, sprinkled with oregano and dressed with a generous amount of extra virgin olive oil.

Nowadays, in Goa, we often eat just a salad for lunch. The serious amount of vitamins that you get with such a meal leaves you with a good feeling. One of my favourite salads is tabbouleh.

1 TABBOULEH

Few herbs deliver as much nutrition as parsley, the base of tabbouleh. This salad originated in the Middle East and has conquered the world just like hummus, baba ghanoush and falafel. On the way, it has morphed from a green salad made mostly with parsley leaves into a salad with bulgur wheat as the main ingredient.

I like to prepare tabbouleh resembling the original. Flat parsley leaves remain the hero of this dish with a strong sidekick of fresh mint. I use cracked wheat sparingly, known in India as daliya. I like to season it with black pepper and za'atar powder, a Middle Eastern spice made from ground thyme, salt, sumac and sesame seeds. Some cooks add coriander leaves, cinnamon and/or other spice mixtures. Tabbouleh makes an excellent side dish for meat or fish. I like it as a main course, a perfect, light lunch on a hot day.

INGREDIENTS

(Serves 4)

- 2-3 bundles flat parsley leaves (about 200 gm or around 3 cups of uncut leaves)
- 1 bundle mint (about 1 cup leaves)
- ½ cup bulgur wheat (daliya)
- 2 big spring onions or several tiny ones
- 3 tomatoes
- 4 tbsp lemon or lime juice
- 8 tbsp extra virgin olive oil
- Salt
- Pepper
- A spice of your choice

METHOD

Wash and dice tomatoes, place into a bowl and add daliya. The moisture from tomatoes and herbs is enough to soften daliya when it sits for half an hour. If you want to serve immediately, mix daliya with three tablespoons hot water.

Wash parsley and mint. Pluck the parsley leaves and cut with a knife. A food processor damages the structure of the leaves. Take a handful of leaves, bundle them with one hand and cut them as finely as possible. Cut mint leaves. Add these herbs to the bowl.

Wash and clean spring onions, slice finely and add to bowl. Add olive oil and lime juice. Season with salt, pepper and other spices.

GO GREEN WITH HERBS

Green herbs are packed with nutrients. Parsley contains vast amounts of vitamin C and A, and folic acid. Parsley's volatile oils help neutralize carcinogens like benzo pyrenes found in smoke from cigarettes and charcoal. It keeps your heart and cardiovascular system healthy and can prevent rheumatic arthritis.

Mint relieves stomach cramps because it relaxes muscles. It is a useful herb in case of indigestion, dyspepsia and irritable bowel syndrome. The phytonutrient monoterpene in mint stops the growth of pancreatic, mammary and liver tumours and protects against cancer in the colon, skin and lungs.

2 RUCOLA/ROCKET/ARUGULA SALAD

This Mediterranean plant, rucola, carries many names. No other green leaf has such a rich, peppery taste that indicates its hidden treasures. It is stuffed with phytonutrients, which prevents cancer, strengthens the immune system and has anti-bacterial and anti-viral properties. Rucola is a good source for folate. It provides a lot of vitamin A, B and C.

It also contains a lot of vitamin K, making it an excellent choice for the elderly. Only 100 grams of rucola delivers 90 per cent of the recommended daily dose of vitamin K, which is crucial for bone formation and healthy brain cells. This plant also contains many minerals, especially iron, copper and potassium.

INGREDIENTS

(Serves 4)

- Any leafy kind of salad
- 1 cup cherry tomatoes or 2 regular tomatoes
- 1 red or yellow bell pepper
- ½ cup basil leaves
- 1 cup rucola/rocket/arugula leaves
- 2 cloves garlic
- 2 tbsp red wine vinegar
- 6 tbsp extra virgin olive oil
- Salt
- Freshly ground pepper

METHOD

Clean salad leaves well. Soak leaves, tomatoes and bell pepper for ten minutes in drinking water that has been mixed with two tablespoons salt. Salt water removes parasites. You can also use a vegetable soap. Drain and rinse.

For vinaigrette, crush garlic with a garlic press. Mix with half a teaspoon salt and vinegar in a glass or container with a tight-fitting lid. Add ground pepper. Mix well. This base helps to emulsify the olive oil later on.

Cut bell pepper into cubes. Halve cherry tomatoes or cube regular tomatoes. Place vegetables and salad leaves into a bowl. Pour olive oil into vinegar mix, close lid and shake well. Proper vinaigrette looks murky – a thick emulsion of oil and vinegar. Pour over salad and mix well. Serve immediately.

☞ **TIP:** The easiest way to make vinaigrette is by using a glass with a tight-closing lid. Put all the ingredients into the glass and then shake. For a dinner party, prepare the vinaigrette in a glass and keep the vegetables in a bowl. When you want to serve the salad, shake the glass; pour the dressing over the salad, mix and serve.

YOU CANNOT EAT TOO MUCH SALAD

I love the taste of fresh basil in vinaigrette mixed with fresh garlic and peppery rucola, all mingling with sweet bell peppers and cherry tomatoes.

You can make this salad with any kind of leaf – lollo rosso, radicchio and iceberg lettuce. My favourite dressing is vinaigrette, the French way with raw garlic. You can also make vinaigrette with honey, mustard, and any fresh herb you desire; even curd or cream or fresh chillies can be used. I take Italian red wine vinegar, sometimes mixing it with balsamic vinegar to enhance its taste. Occasionally, I serve a 'naughty salad' for lunch: I chop a packet of smoked bacon, fry it until crispy and then add garlic and two tablespoons vinegar. A can of tuna and a handful of capers in vinegar also turn this salad into a main course.

VEIL OF GREY

After I had received an award for my first cookbook, I had every reason to be happy, yet life was a struggle. Nothing seemed to give me joy. I felt like life was passing by and everybody had struck it better than me. Everybody seemed to have more money, more fun, more everything. Pre-menopause held me in its throes. When I went to a gynaecologist, he sent me home with an anti-depressant.

I felt the effect instantly. The veil of grey lifted. Suddenly, life was worth living again. I was singing in the car. But I did not want to get used to swallowing a pill every morning. I decided to investigate cooking for happiness and natural mood-enhancing substances in herbs and plants.

One of my all-time favourites is avocado. During avocado season, my husband and I often share one. We halve it and scoop out the flesh with a spoon. When I feel more sophisticated, I prepare guacamole.

3 GUACAMOLE

Guacamole dates back to the Aztecs. When the Spanish arrived in Mexico, guacamole was part of the native menu. You can enjoy it with bread, crackers or vegetable sticks. You can serve it as a starter or as a light main course.

Like rucola, avocado is full of nutrients. The challenge of this dish is finding the perfect avocado. Some avocados have a hard shell. They should show an even colour, ranging from dark green to dark brown, without blemishes or mould. Avocados with soft skin should lightly yield to your touch. You can ripen avocados at home. Cover them with paper, store them in a warm place and check them daily.

INGREDIENTS

(Serves 4)

- 1 big, ripe avocado (around 500 gm)
- 1 yellow or red bell pepper
- 1 bunch parsley
- 5 fresh green chillies
- 2 big cloves garlic
- 2 tbsp lemon or lime juice
- 5 tbsp olive oil
- Salt
- Pepper

METHOD

Crush garlic cloves, place into a bowl and squeeze lemons over it. Add half a teaspoon salt and pepper and stir.

Wash bell pepper, cut into cubes and place in a bowl. Wash and slice fresh chillies. Wash parsley, remove stems and chop leaves. Add to bowl. Halve avocado, remove seed, cut flesh into cubes and add to bowl.

Mix olive oil with garlic in lemon juice, pour dressing over vegetables and mix. Add seasoning as per your taste. Refrigerate guacamole for one hour before serving.

AVOCADO – HEALTHY FAT

The avocado tree has been cultivated in Central and South America since 8000 BC. Avocados provide oleic acid, a monounsaturated fat that helps reduce 'bad' cholesterol levels and lowers the risk of breast cancer. They contain lutein, enabling the body to absorb nutrition from other sources. If you add avocado to your salad, your body can make greater use of the nutrients in it.

Their vitamin E boosts the immune system, keeps the skin healthy and prevents heart disease. They also offer magnesium, vitamins C and B6, folate, iron, and potassium, a mineral that helps regulate blood pressure.

HAPPY MAKERS FROM THE KITCHEN

We all know that good, comforting food has the ability to enhance your mood. When I started researching how to influence mood with food, my son and I were diagnosed with food allergies. Then I wrote a cookbook for allergic people instead. Later, I went back to my happiness project. Food influences our mood enormously but its effects are subtle and take time to manifest. The less processed food you eat, the better you feel. When you avoid processed food, sugar and alcohol, you will feel a change in about two weeks.

While learning about vitamins, I discovered some shocking facts. I knew that natural vitamins are superior to synthetic ones, but I had no idea what really set them apart. For example, vitamin C is not the only ascorbic acid that you find in the synthetic version. Real vitamin C contains many other ingredients like rutin, bioflavonoids and tyrosinase. The industry has little interest in spreading this knowledge. I don't know how many vitamin pills I have consumed in my life, thinking that I did something good for my body.

Even though our food may be polluted, vitamins from natural sources dwarf artificial ones. One of the most common vegetables, the humble cabbage, offers a wealth of nutrition.

4 CABBAGE AND CARROT SALAD

This Greek salad adds a lively dash of colour to your table. To make raw cabbage easier to digest, slice it as finely as possible. You can replace the white with red cabbage. The rich colour of red cabbage reflects its higher concentration of phytonutrients.

INGREDIENTS

(Serves 4)

- ½ medium sized cabbage
- 2 big carrots
- 2 tbsp red wine vinegar
- 5 tbsp olive oil
- Salt
- Pepper

METHOD

Remove outer leaves and trunk from cabbage. Slice finely and place in a bowl.

Clean and grate carrots. Add to bowl. Pour vinegar and olive oil over vegetables, season with salt and pepper, and mix.

This salad can do with variations. Add seeds or nuts of your choice for that extra crunch. For some zing use finely chopped fresh chillies.

CABBAGE KEEPS CANCER AT BAY

Sturdy, abundant and cheap, cabbage is cultivated in the Himalayan valleys, plains of Bavaria and fields in the USA. Groups of Celtic wanderers probably brought the wild cabbage to Europe around 600 BC. Studies show that cruciferous vegetables like cabbage contain a lot of cancer-fighting phytonutrients. They lower our risk of cancer more effectively than any other vegetable. By eating three to five cups of cabbage a week you can lower the risk of cancer by around 30 per cent. Scientists continue to discover phytonutrients all the time. If a vegetable has a strong colour or smell, it indicates a high content of phytonutrients. To make the most of your cabbage, chop it and then let it sit for around ten minutes before cooking it lightly or eating it as a salad. This oxidation increases its nutritional value.

WHAT'S THE TRUTH?

The older I get, the more I become aware that belief and instincts carry the same weight as information, especially when it comes to food. I grew up with the warning to not eat too many eggs because of high cholesterol in them. Nowadays, experts recommend eating eggs often because they contain a wealth of nutrition. Many things that were propagated as scientific truth have been overruled later on.

Around 1950, chemical companies started to produce synthetic vitamins. Today, synthetic vitamin supplements are added to processed foods, prescribed by doctors and taken as over-the-counter medicine. One of the first to recognize the concept of vitamin activity was the controversial Dr Royal Lee, also called the father of holistic nutrition. He was born in 1895 in Wisconsin, USA, and studied to become a dentist. During the course of his life, he secured over seventy US patents for inventions, which brought him financial independence.

His main interest lay in nutrition. He claimed that vitamins were complex groups of interdependent compounds that could only be made by living organisms. According to Dr Lee, a true vitamin could only be obtained from whole, unprocessed foods. The food industry and the US Food and Drug Administration (FDA) opposed his work. They were on a different course at the time, advertising cigarettes as digestive aid. Elmer Nelson, the head of the FDA Nutrition division, said in 1949: 'It is wholly unscientific to state that a well-fed body is more able to resist disease than a less-well-fed body.'

I don't know the truth but I tend to trust Dr Lee. Most synthetic vitamins are made from petroleum extracts, coal tar derivatives and sugars processed with industrial chemicals such as formaldehyde.

I am sure that eating vegetables does more good than harm. Spinach belongs to the dark, leafy greens that should not be missing in any diet. You can just wilt it in the pan together with a bit of olive oil, some spring onions and crushed garlic. If you feel adventurous, try this recipe.

5 SPINACH AND MUSHROOM SALAD

Spinach leaves are an unusual choice for a salad. Combined with button mushrooms and basil, it delivers a tasty dose of vitamins, minerals and phytonutrients. It works well as a side dish with any meat or fish. You can elevate it to a main dish by adding feta and walnuts. But you have to serve this salad immediately. Neither spinach nor mushrooms bear standing around.

INGREDIENTS

(Serves 4)

- 2 cups spinach leaves
- 2 cups white button mushrooms
- ½ cup basil leaves
- 1 clove garlic
- 1 tbsp red wine vinegar
- 1 tbsp balsamic vinegar
- 4 tbsp extra virgin olive oil
- Salt
- Pepper

METHOD

Wash and clean spinach leaves. Rinse and clean mushrooms. Never soak fresh mushrooms in water because they turn mushy.

Wash and clean basil. Place vegetables in a bowl. Crush garlic and put it into a glass with a tight-fitting lid. Add vinegar, salt and pepper. Close lid and shake. Add olive oil and shake well again.

Pour dressing over salad and mix. Serve immediately.

SPINACH FOR HEALTHY BONES

One cup of fresh spinach leaves contains double the amount of vitamin K – vital for our bones – that an adult needs per day. Eating spinach helps maintain a healthy heart, a well-functioning brain and good eyesight.

Green fruits and vegetables like avocado, green beans, peas and spinach display their colour thanks to a high content of chlorophyll. The green colour indicates vitamin C and B, calcium, folate, and fibre. It also shows that the vegetable or fruit contains carotenoids, which boost the immune system, prevent cancer, lower blood pressure and keep your eyes healthy.

☞ **WARNING:** People suffering from hepatitis, rheumatism, and gastric and intestinal inflammations should not eat spinach. The oxalic acid in spinach may worsen their condition.

NEW KIDS ON THE BLOCK

After the divorce from my first husband in 1992, I needed a break. At that time I was working as an editor for a newspaper in Regensburg, Bavaria. I decided to buy an Enfield Bullet and drive through India, although I could not ride a motorbike. It took me two years to prepare for my sabbatical.

In 1994, I arrived in Goa with an army bike. The Bullet scared the hell out of me and its engine never sprang to life in the first try. Thanks to my stubborn nature, I eventually befriended my Bullet. I also met my Italian husband through the bike.

During this period of my life I lived on restaurant fare. After a few months, I developed a rash in my chest area. I thought it was prickly heat; I dabbed it with calamine lotion, but it kept spreading. I could not take it any more. A doctor immediately gave me an injection of vitamin B. After one week of taking (synthetic) vitamin B, I was free from the rash.

But vitamins are not the only components found in fruits and vegetables. Biochemicals like phytonutrients guard the plant against viruses and bacteria, and repel bugs and predators. Phytonutrients appear to serve three major functions in the human body: they act as antioxidants, they regulate hormone levels, and they eliminate toxins. Some phytonutrients smell strongly like the glucosinolates found in broccoli, cauliflower and horseradish.

Broccoli is one vegetable that we should eat frequently.

6 STIR-FRIED BROCCOLI

Both my men, my husband and my son, need persuasion to eat their cruciferous vegetables. My husband wrinkles his nose when he detects a hint of sulphuric odour. The Asian flavours of this dish mask the scent of cabbage. This recipe combines broccoli with red bell pepper. I don't mind only stir-frying the broccoli for around two minutes. You can steam the broccoli for two minutes before stir-frying to soften it without damaging the vitamins.

INGREDIENTS

(Serves 4)

- 2 cups broccoli (one big or two smaller heads)
- 1 big red bell pepper
- 6 spring onions
- 3 cloves garlic

- 1 tbsp minced ginger
- ½ tbsp sesame oil
- 1 tbsp extra virgin olive oil
- 2 tbsp soy sauce
- Salt
- Pepper

METHOD

Clean, wash and chop spring onions. Crush garlic. Wash bell pepper and broccoli. Slice bell pepper and divide broccoli into small florets. If you want to steam broccoli to soften it, do this now. Clean and mince ginger root.

Place ingredients within easy reach before you start stir-frying. Heat olive oil in a wok. Slide onions, ginger and garlic into wok and stir until onions have turned translucent. Add bell pepper, soy sauce and sesame oil and mix.

Add broccoli and fry for two minutes. If you want to add some zing in this dish, add chopped fresh chillies. Season vegetables with salt and pepper before serving.

BROCCOLI

Broccoli contains generous amounts of vitamins and minerals. Its outstanding quality is its combination of vitamins, minerals, flavonoids and carotenoids that help eradicate toxins. Our bodies get rid of toxins in a two-step process. Broccoli supports both of these steps through its three different glucosinolates. It is the only vegetable that offers these important phytonutrients in this combination and concentration.

Broccoli fights chronic inflammation and cancer. It has an unusually strong combination of both, vitamin A and K. For people who lack vitamin D, broccoli is a food they should eat as often as possible. It is also a rich source of a flavonoid called kaempferol that fights cancer cells.

ANTIOXIDANTS, FREE RADICALS AND VITAMINS

I love the word 'free radicals' because I am a rebel at heart. I was born with the family name Rebel. As a girl sandwiched between two brothers I had to stand up for myself.

Free radicals are unstable atoms that miss an electron in their outer shell. This happens naturally during metabolism in the body. Pollution, radiation and smoking can also produce a lot of free radicals. They 'rob' the missing electron from the next possible atom, crippling them to fix their atomic structure. This damages cells and tissues. Antioxidants provide missing electrons to free radicals and neutralise them before they can harm your body. Vitamin-rich ingredients are usually bursting with antioxidants.

I grew up in a Bavarian Catholic family. Every Sunday we went to the church. Both my parents were public servants but my mother had given up work to raise kids. She ran her household like a well-oiled machine. We children knew exactly what chores we had to do. My mother cooked mostly traditional German fare. A hot meal was served at lunchtime to the family. My father came home from office to join us. After lunch, we usually had a piece of fruit, 'to eat enough vitamins', as my mother used to say.

Vitamins keep cells strong. They help form tissue structure

and fight infections. We get most vitamins from our food except vitamin D. Our bodies produce vitamin D when they are exposed to sunlight. Vitamins are grouped into two categories: fat-soluble and water-soluble. The fat-soluble vitamins – A, D, E and K – can be stored in the fatty tissues of our bodies.

We need to ingest water-soluble B and C vitamins daily to meet our needs. If we eat too many, they leave our bodies with urine. There is one exception: vitamin B12 can be stored in the liver for many years. The group of B vitamins help to release the energy from the food we eat and promote metabolism. They detoxify organs, stabilize the functions of the nervous system, and keep skin, eyes and hair healthy. Vitamin C fights infections, strengthens blood vessels and destroys free radicals. It helps the body absorb iron and maintain tissue. It also promotes wound healing.

In recent years, the raw food diet has become fashionable. I believe it might be great to lose weight but I consider this approach to food too radical. We don't belong to the plant-eating species. Nature has designed humans to eat everything. Eating vegetables and fruits raw is not always the best way to absorb nutrients. For example, our bodies digest the potent red antioxidant lycopene from tomatoes better when it is cooked. Many vegetables like carrots release nutrients better after cooking them.

COOK WITH LITTLE WATER

When dealing with vitamins, remember the following: fat-soluble vitamins A, E and D are not destroyed by water but bond with fat. Avoid using huge amounts of oil or butter while frying. Eat the fat you use to fry your food. Don't throw it out! Of course this does not apply to deep-frying.

All other vitamins are water-soluble. When food touches water, vitamins leach out. Never soak vegetables and fruits, rinse them. When cooking vegetables, use as little water and cook them as short as possible. Don't cut the vegetables very small so that there is less exposure to air and water. Steaming or cooking vegetables in the pressure cooker preserves most vitamins. Always cover the pot so vitamins don't escape into air. Some experts recommend the use of griddle pan because then you don't need long cooking hours.

7 BRUSSELS SPROUTS IN GARLIC BUTTER

Steamed Brussels sprouts bind better with bile acids than raw or cooked ones, lowering cholesterol levels. This vegetable is extremely healthy but its flavour needs a strong counterpoint like crispy fried garlic in butter. In India, Brussels sprouts are quite rare. Whenever I find them in the market, I buy as much as possible and freeze whatever I don't prepare immediately.

INGREDIENTS

(Serves 4)

- 30 Brussels sprouts (4 cups or so)
- 10 garlic cloves

- 5 tbsp butter
- 2 tbsp sesame seeds
- Salt
- Pepper

METHOD

Clean Brussels sprouts and halve them. Wash and let sit for ten minutes. This helps to develop their healthy components. Crush garlic. For steaming, I use a foldable stainless steel inset that fits into any pot. Place hot water under steamer, add Brussels sprouts, close lid and steam for five to ten minutes. Melt butter in a small pan. Fry garlic over medium heat until golden and crispy. Be careful not to brown it too much. Toss Brussels sprouts in garlic butter, season with salt and pepper and sprinkle with sesame seeds.

BRUSSELS SPROUTS TOP CHARTS

This vegetable tops the nutrition charts in many regards. Brussels sprouts contain more glucosinolates that prevent cancer than any other cruciferous vegetable. They also contain huge amounts of vitamins and minerals. One cup of Brussels sprouts delivers more than double the amount of vitamin K you need daily, and more than your daily need of vitamin C. Vitamin K is important for healthy bones and proper blood circulation. It also has serious amounts of folate, manganese, vitamins like B6 and other minerals. Its origins go back to the 16th century to a region near Brussels, hence the name.

BE BODY WISE

In the grip of anorexia nervosa during my teenage years, I read lists of calorie contents like novels. In the eighties you could only learn the amount of calories. Nowadays, nutrition facts – serving sizes, calories, vitamin and mineral content etc. – are printed on every packaged item you buy. I read them with interest but refuse to add similar information to my recipes. I believe that we should listen to our bodies instead of counting calories and measuring the food on our plates.

Our bodies have an inborn wisdom. They communicate with our mind through subtle hints that manifest as cravings and appetites. Your body tells you what is missing. If you stick to a diet, subtle hints are ignored. A diet may be well-balanced and meet the needs of your body according to scientific knowledge. That does not mean your body submits to these standards.

The perfect way to stay fit and slim cannot be found in books or the Internet. We have to take matters into our own hands and trust our appetites and cravings. I don't mean to abuse food as emotional band-aid. There is nothing wrong with indulging in chocolates or ice creams once in a while but, stuffing yourself is sickening. If you have an eating disorder, do get professional help.

A psychotherapist helped me discover the reasons behind my obsession with food. After one year of weekly sessions I was cured of trying to stuff myself with food. Now I am able to really enjoy food. One of my favourite dishes is gazpacho, a Spanish classic.

When you hear soup, a steaming bowl comes to mind.

Gazpacho is the opposite – a cold, thick vegetable cream. Some claim it dates back to the Romans, others say the Moors brought it to Spain. Originally, gazpacho was a simple dish made with bread and olive oil. In modern times it has evolved into a variety of concoctions.

8 GAZPACHO

INGREDIENTS

(Serves 12)

- 1 kg red tomatoes
- 500 gm green peppers
- 3 medium-sized cucumbers
- 500 gm bread, best whole wheat toast
- 1 packet tomato puree
- 10 tbsp olive oil
- 5 big cloves garlic
- Salt
- Pepper
- Bread to make croutons
- Spring onions

METHOD

Put tomatoes for a minute into boiling water. Skin them and remove seeds. Trash the flesh. Remove crust from bread and soak the bread in a bit of water. Add softened bread to tomatoes.

Wash, deseed peppers and cut into pieces. Skin and deseed

cucumbers and cut into pieces. Crush garlic. Add vegetables to bowl. Add salt, pepper, olive oil and tomato puree.

Make a smooth paste with a blender. Gazpacho should have a creamy consistency.

Chill it in the fridge for two hours. To make croutons, cut bread into square pieces, place pieces on a cookie sheet and toast in oven. Serve gazpacho with croutons and chopped spring onions.

GARLIC – A DIVINE INGREDIENT

One ingredient that I cannot cook without is garlic. Ancient Egyptians worshipped it and Greek athletes used to chew it. Studies confirm that garlic contains powerful antioxidants. Garlic is a powerful antibiotic, reduces blood pressure, balances cholesterol levels and prevents Alzheimer's disease and dementia. Exposing garlic for ten minutes to air after crushing makes its healthy components heat resistant.

FOR FREEDOM AND FUN

Another reason why I refuse serving sizes and calorie contents is of practical nature. I don't feel like measuring my meals in cups nor do I want to impart to my family this restrictive approach. I have added generous serving sizes to my recipes to give you an idea about amounts. They should not be taken literally. The beauty of cooking is that you have the freedom to do what you like. I understand recipes as guidelines, not as rules written in stone.

At meal times we eat as much as we want, sometimes even

second and third helpings. Maybe sometimes we overeat a little, but who cares? I believe measuring your food takes the fun out of eating. Our meals should be sources of joy and pleasure. In our daily life we use our brains so much; meal times should be dedicated to sensations and good feelings.

When we eat a diet with a lot of variety, good quality ingredients and plenty of vegetables and fruits, we should be well-nourished, and will not need to over-analyse our meals.

The following recipe uses a giant vegetable that delivers a wealth of nutrition and is easy to prepare. Even cleaning it takes little time.

9　PUMPKIN SOUP

Some years ago, my son joined an international school in Goa. For Halloween, the school organized a pumpkin carving competition. Being German, I had not used pumpkin in my cooking. The contest changed this. As a novice at carving, I bought two big pumpkins that left me with a mountain of flesh.

Pumpkin soup seemed to be the easiest solution. The result was surprisingly delicious. After I researched its nutritional properties, I felt a bit silly that I had ignored this great vegetable.

INGREDIENTS

(Serves 10-12)

🍃 2 kg pumpkin flesh (a medium pumpkin)
🍃 5 big onions

- 5 cloves garlic
- 2 carrots
- 1 stalk celery
- 2 medium potatoes
- 1 tbsp oregano
- 8 tbsp extra virgin olive oil
- 4 cups vegetable stock
- Salt
- Pepper

METHOD

You need a big pressure cooker or pot. Clean vegetables and cut into pieces. Add stock – any kind is fine but avoid cubes with monosodium glutamate (MSG). Cook for ten minutes on low flame after the first whistle. In a normal pot, cook until vegetables soften.

Add olive oil and oregano. Blend vegetables to a smooth puree. Season with salt and pepper.

PUMPKIN GOES A LONG WAY

Pumpkins belong to the family of cucurbitaceous fruits like cucumber, squash and melons. Archaeological evidence shows that pumpkins were already cultivated 5000 years ago in China and Mexico. Pumpkin is low in calories and high in nutrition. Only 100 grams provide more than double your daily requirement of vitamin A. It also has plenty of vitamin C, E and various Bs, and minerals like copper, calcium, potassium and phosphorus. The yellow or orange colour of the flesh shows its high content of phytonutrients like carotenes and lutein. It also provides a lot of dietary fibre that keeps your intestines going.

COMMUNICATION IS KEY

Everything depends on communication; also our body, a sophisticated organism steered by biochemical and bioelectrical processes. There is still a lot to discover but one thing is sure: the fuel for our bodies comes from food. We are what we eat. It is easier to feel good when our bodies are well-fed. Feelings are produced in the brain and depend on the communication network inside our bodies.

Scientists have developed the term 'NEI Super System' to describe the interaction in our bodies. NEI stands for Nervous, Endocrine and Immune, and consists of three different systems that communicate with each other.

1. The brain, the spinal cord and all the nerves make up the nervous system.
2. The endocrine system regulates the body's growth, metabolism and sexual functions with the help of hormones.
3. The immune system protects the body from invaders with the help of antibodies.

Antibodies travel in the blood stream and transport messages. The nervous system works with neurotransmitters that remain in and around nerve cells. Some hormones act as neurotransmitters; they transmit signals to nerve cells all over the body.

Without communication, our body would not know what to do. Without vitamins, our body cannot synthesize hormones and neurotransmitters. The following recipe delivers hot and fresh char grilled zucchini and aubergines in a few minutes.

10 VEGETABLES FROM THE GRIDDLE

I keep praising my griddle pan. It mimics the effects of a charcoal grill without the hustle. One easy way to prepare an impressive side dish is by slicing zucchini and aubergines, coating them in olive oil and roasting them on the griddle pan.

INGREDIENTS

(Serves 4)

- 2 medium zucchini
- 1 big aubergine
- 6 tbsp olive oil
- 2 tbsp lemon juice
- Salt
- Pepper
- ½ cup parsley
- ½ cup mint

METHOD

Wash zucchini and aubergine and cut into slices about half a centimetre thick. Place into a bowl and coat with two tablespoons oil.

Heat griddle pan over medium fire. Place vegetable slices on pan and fry them until they have brown stripes on both sides.

Place on a plate and sprinkle with salt and pepper. Wash herbs, chop roughly and spread over slices.

Put lemon juice into a glass with a tight-fitting lid. Add salt and pepper. Shake, add olive oil and shake well again. Drizzle dressing over vegetables and serve immediately.

SUPERFOOD AUBERGINES

Aubergines or eggplants are an excellent source of potassium. This mineral helps regulate salt levels, and is responsible for the hydration of our tissues and body cells. It also plays an important role in transmitting signals along neurons.

Aubergines contain a lot of vitamins and minerals like vitamin B6, folate, magnesium and niacin as well as copper, manganese and thiamine (vitamin B1). Aubergines also have the potent antioxidant nasunin, which blocks the formation of free radicals.

BALANCE IS EVERYTHING

Our body resembles a family living together. Every part of the body influences each other. Imagine a waiter trying to balance three trays loaded with dishes. The three NEI communication systems perform this act all the time. Imbalances affect our feelings and moods.

The different parts of our brain, the limbic, the cerebellum and the brain stem, communicate with the prefrontal cortex through feelings. The brain stem processes the information from our senses. Relevant bits go to the limbic system that creates feelings.

That's why it is so important to follow cravings and appetites: our brain expresses what the body needs. Interestingly, many of our vegetarian guests have started to eat meat at our dinner table. Pasta with bacon or the following chicken liver pâté often makes them forget their vegetarian lifestyle.

Vegetarians tend to lack vitamin B12. This vitamin is only found in animal products and plays an essential role in the manufacture of red blood cells, the function of nerve cells and replicating DNA.

11 CHICKEN LIVER PÂTÉ

I added chicken liver pâté to my recipes of vitamin bombs to point out the importance of vitamin B12. Only meat, seafood and dairy products deliver vitamin B12 that can be stored for years in the human liver.

A lack of this vitamin leads to anaemia, loss of balance, numbness or tingling in the arms and legs, skin rashes and weakness. Our bodies need vitamin B12 to produce the coating of our neurons, essential to transfer signals between nerve cells. A lack of vitamin B12 can lead to senility.

Because vitamin B12 is water-soluble, it is important how you prepare chicken liver pâté. Never soak liver in water. I marinate it for several days in brandy, garlic and thyme and then cook it in the marinade. I always prepare a lot and freeze portions.

INGREDIENTS

(Makes 1 kg)

- 500 gm chicken liver
- 500 gm salted butter
- 200 ml brandy
- 10 cloves garlic
- ½ cup fresh thyme
- 3 tbsp extra virgin olive oil
- Salt
- Pepper

METHOD

Remove veins from chicken livers and chop into pieces. Place in a container. Crush garlic, wash thyme and add with brandy. Close container and marinate liver overnight.

Bring butter to room temperature. Heat olive oil in a pan and add chicken livers with marinade. Fry over medium heat until liquid has evaporated. Let it cool down. Pick out stalks of thyme.

Put liver into a blender and add soft butter. Blend to smooth puree and season with salt and pepper.

CHICKEN LIVER SUPPORTS CELLS

Chicken liver not only contains vitamin B12, but also folic acid or vitamin B9. Folic acid is needed for a strong immune system, DNA synthesis, cell growth and the formation of red blood cells and amino acids. It also assists digestion, improves mental and emotional health, and is important for healthy cell division and replication. Diarrhoea, heartburn and constipation can indicate lack of folic acid.

Adequate amounts of folic acid are especially important for pregnant women. Beef, chicken liver and leafy green vegetables such as broccoli, collards, chard, spinach, and romaine lettuce, provide folic acid.

12 SIMPLE GRANITA OR SORBET

Sorbet is ice cream made with fruits, water and sugar. It's a great way to imbibe a serious dose of vitamins and minerals. My recipe contains little sugar. Sugar consumes B vitamins during digestion, plays yoyo with blood sugar levels and makes you fat. I believe a bit of sugar is OK. Sugar substitutes tend to have drawbacks too.

Preparing sorbet and granita is easy with an ice cream machine. Without it, it takes some effort and time. The difference between granita and sorbet lies in the presentation. Sorbet is served like ice cream while granita is forked into shards and served in a glass with a straw.

INGREDIENTS

(Serves 4)

- 1 kg fruits
- 2 tbsp lemon juice
- 3 tbsp sugar
- 100 ml water

METHOD

Boil sugar with water and let it cool. Clean fruit and puree in a blender. Combine fruit puree with syrup and lemon juice and refrigerate overnight. If you own an ice cream machine, churn fruit until sorbet is done. Store in a container in the freezer. Thaw a bit before serving.

If you don't have an ice cream maker, pour fruit mixture into a tray, cover with cling film and freeze it.

After forty-five minutes, scrape ice crystals from sides into middle of tray. Cover again and return to freezer. Repeat this process at least two more times.

For granita, thaw sorbet, scrape it with a fork and serve in tall glasses with a straw.

> ☞ **TIP:** You can use any kind of fruit to make sorbet and granita. Strawberries are great, pineapple and watermelon are also good. The traditional Italian sorbet is made with lemon juice.

DELIGHT FROM DECADENT ROME

Sorbet dates back a long time. The Romans appreciated this refreshment. The emperor Nero, who set Rome afire, organized runners to pass buckets of snow from the mountains to his banquet hall. His sorbet was made with honey and wine.

Marco Polo returned to Italy from his travels to China with recipes combining snow, juice and fruit pulp. Catherine de Medici brought frozen desserts to France in 1533 when she married the Duke of Orleans. By the 17th century, everybody in Europe had learnt about sorbets. The French started to use sorbets as a palate cleanser between courses.

BIOCHEMICALS AND FEELINGS

How we feel depends on bio chemicals in our brains – and the level of nourishment we imbibe with our diet. Food is a collection of bio chemicals that affects our state of mind even before it reaches our mouth. The sight and smell of food can make us salivate and excite a horde of feelings: desire and guilt, appetite, hunger, happiness ... how we use food depends on us.

Fruit salad can invoke many feelings, but guilt is not one of them. We all know we should eat as many vegetables and fruits as possible. I like a bit of texture and taste, delivered by walnuts, lemon juice and homemade vanilla extract.

13 FRUIT SALAD

Growing up in the 1970s, I have seen many versions of fruit salad. For German housewives, fruit salad meant removing the lid from a tin of fruits, an easy way to serve fruits in wintertime.

For me, fruit salad means fresh produce of the season.

INGREDIENTS

(Serves 4)

- 1 kg fruits, any kind you like and find fresh
- 100 gm walnuts or any other kind of nuts you like

- 3 tbsp lemon juice
- 3 tbsp homemade vanilla extract

METHOD

Wash and cut all fruits. Place in a bowl and mix with lemon juice. Add vanilla extract and chopped nuts.

You can prepare fruit salad a few hours before you want to serve it.

VANILLA – A SPICE FROM MEXICO

Few spices stimulate our gastric juices like vanilla does. The first artificial vanilla extracts were synthesized in the late 19th century, based on pine bark and clove oil. Today most artificial vanilla is made from petrochemicals. Imitation never equals the real thing.

Cortez brought vanilla from Mexico to Europe. For a long time, Mexico was the only producer of vanilla because only a Mexican bee can pollinate the vanilla flower, which produces the pod. In 1819 French entrepreneurs managed to pollinate the flowers by hand. Thanks to this technique many spice farmers in tropical regions started to produce vanilla.

GO WITH YOUR INSTINCTS

Our modern world tends to be hugely complicated and frightening. Thanks to the Internet we have access to a lot of information. But who tells us what is right and what is wrong? How can we know which information to trust?

Today, more than ever, we should trust our instincts. After reading my way through many books and websites, I doubt everybody, especially when it comes to vitamins. Most of the websites condemning synthetic vitamins sell expensive whole-food vitamins. Many of them claim that the soil nowadays is so poor that our food hardly contains vitamins any more.

I do believe that pesticides and chemical fertilisers have reduced the quality of farm soil and that food is polluted. But many seem to exaggerate this to sell their products. I refuse to listen to these prophets of doom. I buy as much organic food as possible and hope that this is slightly less polluted than regular products. I eat as many vegetables and fruits as possible and I can assure you that it makes a difference.

CHAPTER 2

BUILDING BLOCKS FOR THE BRAIN

Our bodies rejoice when we feed them well. Food can change our state of mind. That does not mean you will be happy all the time but it will be easier to overcome bad moments and face your problems. We all grapple with frustrations in everyday life. It depends on us if we let problems put us down or if we face them head on.

Our brains determine the way we feel, act and behave. They are made from neurons. These neurons need neurotransmitters to communicate with each other. Neurotransmitter levels in our brain influence our mood directly. Lack of neurotransmitters causes many mental disorders, the most common being depression.

In recent years, a lot of therapies have been developed to improve levels of neurotransmitters, like the amino acid therapy, TMG supplements and many others. The aim of these therapies is to balance neurotransmitter levels in the brain with the help of pills or restrictive diets.

I don't know how well this works because I have not tried any. However, I have experienced the benefits of a proper diet. I feel a lot better now than five years ago and I know a lot more about nutrition. I believe if you are not suicidal, you might want to consider treating depression with healthy food before spending a lot of money on questionable therapies or risk getting addicted to pills.

Neurotransmitter molecules are too big to pass through the blood-brain barrier. Only amino acids, the components of proteins, can cross over. This makes expensive pills with neurotransmitters quite useless.

We need good, home cooked food with proteins to synthesize neurotransmitters. All neurotransmitters are put together from amino acids, the components of proteins. That means we need to eat plenty of proteins to furnish the building blocks for neurotransmitters. But we also need vitamin B6 and B12, to manufacture neurotransmitters. Electrolytes like potassium, sodium, calcium and omega-3 fatty acids play a crucial role too.

FREE AS A BIRD

Our brains change according to our experiences, thoughts and feelings. When depression had coloured my world a sad grey, my first step towards a happier life was the conscious decision to be happy.

Falling in love with my first husband had convinced me that the world could be paradise. An awakening followed when my husband turned out quite flawed. Another great period of my life was my journey on an Enfield Bullet through

India. After divorce, I had thrown off all responsibilities.

I was lonely and unhappy because of my divorce. But I loved the sound of the engine, and opening the throttle and blasting away, wind in my hair. I loved arriving at roadside 'dhabas' and everybody staring in awe at the lone woman rider. Today I see many young Indian women riding motorbikes and that fills me with hope. The world needs strong women.

Being in love with my Italian husband lasted two whole years. I was more aware of human nature and made room for character flaws. Nothing prepared me for the joy of motherhood. When I first held my son in my arms, life transformed. The grey morass of depression had made me forget the good times. Somehow, all joy had left me. I believe neurotransmitter levels in my brain were seriously out of balance.

Chicken delivers complete proteins; it contains all nine amino acids that are vital for the human metabolism and for synthesising neurotransmitters. Roasted chicken remains my favourite chicken recipe because it takes little time to prepare.

14 ROASTED CHICKEN

Few dishes are as forgiving and convenient as a bird coupled with potatoes. If you have to watch your weight, cook two chickens and forget about the potatoes. Serve it with a salad that includes dark, leafy greens. You can use chicken leftovers in salads or sandwiches.

I prefer rosemary and garlic as main aromatics in this dish. If you want, you can add quartered onions, bell peppers or any kind of vegetable.

INGREDIENTS

(Serves 4)

- 1 chicken (around 1 kg)
- 4 tbsp olive oil
- 1 kg potatoes
- 10 cloves garlic
- Dried or fresh rosemary
- Salt
- Pepper

METHOD

Clean chicken and rub skin with salt; grind black pepper over it. If you have brined your chicken, drain it, but do not rinse or salt. Put rosemary and one garlic clove into belly.

Peel potatoes and cut into pieces. Spread olive oil over bottom of a baking dish. Place chicken inside with breast facing down. Add potatoes, remaining garlic and one glass water.

Cook for around one and a half hours at 180 degrees Celsius. Occasionally, baste chicken with juices collecting.

When you prick chicken with a skewer, juices should be colourless.

☞ **TIP:** Brining improves roasted chicken. You need a container big enough to place the chicken. For brine, dissolve ¼ cup of salt in two litres water. Submerse the chicken in the brine and keep it overnight in the fridge.

ROSEMARY – DEW OF THE SEA

The silver green needles of rosemary deliver Mediterranean flavour. The Latin name of rosemary means 'dew of the sea'. This woody herb beautifully grows close to the beach and forms bushes up to two metres high.

Its aromatic oils enhance memory and help prevent cancer, boost liver functions and put off age-related skin damage. For me, rosemary's most important quality is the wonderful aroma. If you can, use fresh rosemary.

MOUNTAIN MAGIC AND ICY WATERS

Although the journey on my Enfield Bullet was exhilarating, I faced utter exhaustion. From Goa I had driven to Manali in Himachal Pradesh, where I took a break. I stayed close to the hot springs in Vashisht with a view of snow-covered Himalayan peaks. Every morning, I soaked my body in warm water.

After some weeks of leisure, I started towards Ladakh. The first obstacle was the Rohtang pass. It snowed heavily but my Enfield pulled through ice and snow heaps. I had just passed the peak of the Rohtang pass when a scooter with two well-fed Sikhs overtook me. One pink and one green turban left me astonished in their wake.

Later on, I had to cross some rivers. Every time, I lost balance on slippery pebbles and the bullet tumbled into ice-cold water. Completely shattered I reached Jispa, a small village surrounded by rugged mountains.

The Kalachakra, a Tibetan Buddhist gathering, was about to take place. Together with some foreigners I rented a tent. A wild mélange of persons had arrived from far and wide to meet the Dalai Lama. Mountain people in brocade vests strutted through the village. Women displayed necklaces with huge turquoises and corals while men had swords dangling from their belts – mountain magic.

Like human beings, our neurons come in many forms and sizes. Neurons transmit signals through electrochemical impulses produced by the exchange of sodium and potassium ions, the essential minerals.

Basil, one of the main ingredients of pesto, is a great source for potassium. Most of us get rather too much sodium from salt. The following recipe delivers proteins with a healthy dose of minerals.

15 CHICKEN-PESTO ROLLS

Many years ago, I wanted to prepare a special dinner for the Italian honorary consul in Goa, Antonio DalNegro, and his wife. Laura DalNegro is one of the best cooks I know. She hails from Liguria, an Italian region known for many delicacies, among them pesto and focaccia, a bread smothered in olive oil.

I hoped to demonstrate my skills with the following dish. It is great for dinner parties because you can prepare it one day in advance. Keep the rolls stuffed with pesto in the fridge. On the day of the dinner, just coat the rolls in flour, fry them and prepare the sauce.

INGREDIENTS

(Serves 4)

- 4 boneless chicken breasts
- Wooden toothpicks
- 5 tbsp pesto
- 1 cup whole wheat flour
- 5 tbsp olive oil
- 3 big, red onions
- 1 cup white wine
- 2 cups chicken or beef stock (or water, if you don't have any stock)

Pesto:

- 3 bundles fresh basil leaves
- ½ cup cashew nuts
- 5 walnuts
- 6 big cloves garlic
- 50 gm parmigiano or grana cheese
- 100 ml olive oil
- Salt
- Pepper

METHOD

You can use commercial or homemade pesto. To prepare pesto, wash and clean basil leaves. Chop cashew and walnuts, and put in a blender. Add leaves, crushed garlic, grated cheese, olive oil, salt and pepper and blend to a smooth paste.

For pesto rolls, carefully slice each chicken breast into two thin pieces and season with salt and pepper. Spread pesto over each slice. Roll pieces with pesto facing inside and secure with toothpicks.

Place flour in a plate and coat rolls. Peel onions and chop finely.

Heat olive oil in a big pan and fry rolls golden brown. Keep aside.

Fry onions in the pan until they start to brown. Add white wine and stock, season with salt and freshly grated pepper.

Let sauce boil for two minutes, then add chicken rolls and simmer on low heat for fifteen minutes.

CHICKEN FOR PROPER METABOLISM

Chicken contains lots of proteins, many vitamins and selenium. This mineral plays a vital role for our metabolism. Eating an abundance of selenium can help fight off cancer too. Niacin, a kind of B vitamin present in chicken meat, is needed to synthesise neurotransmitters.

When you buy frozen chicken, check that it does not show any ice crystals or freezer burn, a whitish discolouring. Refuse frozen chicken in torn plastic cover.

16 SURPRISE BURGERS

I developed the recipe for surprise burgers after returning from holidays in the USA. The turkey and chicken burgers there had been a disappointment. Many of them arrived burnt, inside a bun with tiny bits of lettuce and tomato, a hopelessly dry affair. Back home, I decided to make it work. For surprise burgers I stuffed chicken mince with thick slices of mozzarella.

These burgers remain juicy thanks to eggs and oats. If you pair them with dark leafy greens and whole wheat rolls, you nourish body and soul, especially your brain.

INGREDIENTS

(Makes 6)

- 500 gm minced chicken meat
- 2 eggs
- 2 cups rolled oats
- 1 packet mozzarella (200 gm)
- 6 tbsp olive oil
- 3 big cloves garlic
- 1 tbsp dried oregano
- Salt
- Pepper

METHOD

Place minced meat into a bowl. Crush garlic. Add with eggs, oats, one tablespoon dried oregano, salt, pepper and three tablespoons olive oil. Combine everything. Cut mozzarella into six slices.

Divide minced meat mix into six equal portions. Wet your hands with water so dough does not stick. Take half of each portion and form a round patty. Press one mozzarella slice into patty and cover with remaining mince. Press borders together; the cheese needs to be covered on all sides. Heat olive oil in a pan and fry burgers slowly. They take about five minutes to turn golden. Serve immediately.

☞ **TIP:** You can easily mince chicken meat in a blender. Clean the meat from fat and sinews; cut into pieces and blend it.

HORMONAL IMBALANCE

As a child, I wanted to be a good girl. I excelled in school. I never refused to dry the dishes. I was desperately trying to make my parents love me more but my father's outbursts kept terrifying me; my mother was so busy I never seemed to win her full affection.

When I reached puberty, the explosion of hormones wreaked havoc in my brain – and nobody noticed. I constantly checked myself in the mirror; my belly and my legs seemed to be of elephantine proportions. I embarked on a mission to starve myself. I only ate tiny portions and chewed every bite a hundred times.

My body was the only space where I could exert control. This upset our family life greatly. A starving teenager can destroy everybody's appetite at the dinner table. Those days, nobody had heard of eating disorders. 'Put some butter on your bread,' was my mother's response to my hunger games.

I guess my neurotransmitter levels were heavily out of balance, and starving made it worse. Problems with neurotransmitters are the base of many psychiatric and neurological disorders. Neurotransmitter levels can be affected through stress, diet, genetic disposition and drugs.

The main feel-good neurotransmitters are dopamine, serotonin, oxytocin and endorphin. But there are many more that are important for the proper functioning of our bodies. Norepinephrine, also called noradrenaline, helps us stay motivated, alert and focussed. In 1994, the most common neurotransmitter of the central nervous system was discovered: glutamate. You may know it as the seasoning, monosodium glutamate. In the brain, glutamate is responsible for learning, memory and cognition. GABA (gamma aminobutyric acid) is another common neurotransmitter, called the brain's Valium. A lack of GABA leads to anxiety disorders, followed by depression.

Acetylcholine, the main carrier of thought and memory, plays a big role in muscle coordination. We need to eat choline, a part of it, because our bodies cannot produce it. One of the best sources of choline is egg yolk. Wheat germ, organ meat and whole wheat products also provide choline. If egg isn't an option, replace it with minced meat. Try the next recipe.

17 ROCKET BURGERS

For years I tried without success to make my son eat salad. Then a friend sent me a recipe for meat loaf loaded with different kinds of vegetables and spices, so I started another attempt. My son ate the burgers fortified with rucola, basil, spring onions and carrots without complaining, although my husband kept asking about the green colour. I avoided answering questions until dinner was over.

INGREDIENTS

(Makes 12)

- 500 gm chicken mince
- 2 cups oats
- 2 tbsp flour
- 2 eggs
- 2 bundles rucola
- 1 bundle basil
- 1 bundle spring onions
- 1 big carrot
- 3 cloves garlic
- 50 gm sesame seeds
- 5 tbsp olive oil
- Salt
- Pepper

METHOD

Wash and clean rucola, basil, spring onions and carrots. Chop vegetables and blend together in a blender. Put into a bowl. Add chicken mince, oats, flour, eggs, crushed garlic, salt and pepper. Combine all ingredients.

Spread olive oil over a cookie sheet. Put sesame seeds on a plate. Form dough into flat, round burgers and coat with sesame seeds. Place onto oiled cookie sheet. Bake at 190 degrees for forty minutes. After twenty minutes flip over. The sesame seeds should turn golden.

BASIL, NATURE'S ASPIRIN

The wonderful basil contains flavonoids that protect cells from damage by radiation and oxygen. It also inhibits the growth of bacteria that have become resistant to antibiotics, and provides relief from inflammation by acting in a similar way to aspirin. This herb also contains vitamin A and C, magnesium, iron, calcium, and potassium.

HAPPY MAKERS AND MOOD BUSTERS

When we feel stressed, many of us rush to trigger happy chemicals to mask the bad feelings, the start of vicious cycles. We need to learn to accept all feelings. It may sound childish, but I experienced an epiphany during a psycho-workshop.

Tears were streaming down my face when the therapist told me that it is OK to feel bad. This simple statement resonated. It is OK to feel bad! We all feel bad, life is hurtful and we cannot avoid bad feelings and stress. Accepting bad feelings is better than suppressing them or masking them with an addiction.

When we experience stress overload constantly, we might want to consider changing our lifestyle. It also helps to understand the nature of our happy-making chemicals to trigger them without side effects.

Always opt for easy solutions. When I need a snack or lunch, chicken-carrot cakes are great.

18 CHICKEN-CARROT CAKES

I suggest a Mediterranean version with dry oregano as the main aroma. You might want to try Asian flavours with sesame oil, soya sauce, grated ginger and garlic. What about using the flavours of the Middle East with za'atar, cumin powder and some tahini? If you want to prepare a vegetarian version, replace the chicken with grated cheese or just do the basic version with carrots, onions, eggs and oats.

INGREDIENTS

(Makes 20)

- 200 gm boneless chicken meat or mince
- 3 eggs
- 3 medium onions
- 3 big cloves garlic
- 3 large carrots
- 3 cups oats
- 6 tbsp olive oil
- 1 tbsp dried oregano
- Salt
- Pepper

METHOD

Cut chicken into pieces and mince in a blender. Spread four tablespoons olive oil over a cookie sheet. Clean onions, garlic and carrots and chop them. Add mince, oats, eggs, oregano, remaining olive oil, one teaspoon salt and pepper.

Blend everything to smooth dough that holds its shape.

Form twenty cake pieces and place onto cookie sheet. I use an ice cream scoop for this. Bake for half an hour at 190 degrees. After twenty minutes, flip over the cakes to let them brown.

DOUBLE-FACED SUBSTANCE

My kitchen is a perfect place to get dopamine fixes. When people appreciate your food, dopamine gets released. Every new recipe poses a challenge. When you add a new dish to your repertoire, you can be proud of your achievement. Along the way you might have done a lot to increase dopamine levels in your brain.

Dopamine, one of the major happy-making neurotransmitters, is a double-faced substance. Because it doles out feelings of accomplishment that pass quickly, it is involved in a lot of addictions. Dopamine is a hormone that plays many different roles in the body. It increases urine output in the kidneys and dilates blood vessels. In the brain, dopamine supports memory, focus, attention and problem-solving. A loss of dopamine-secreting neurons causes Parkinson's disease. The amount of dopamine diminishes quickly when you repeat an action often. This effect is called habituation.

Many drugs work with dopamine receptors in the brain. Cocaine and amphetamines increase dopamine in the synaptic cleft. Drugs and unhealthy habits easily lead to vicious cycles. If you are stuck in a vicious cycle you need to rewire your brain. The ability of our brain to develop new synapses is known as plasticity. When you are a teenager, this happens easily. For an adult, it takes longer but it is possible. Some synapses start growing after twenty minutes of a stimulating activity.

While learning about our happy makers, I have started to pat myself on the shoulder. This is a self-congratulatory step that makes you feel good. Nobody needs to know about it. You can divide every task into baby steps and tell yourself: 'Bravo, you did it, one step closer to your goal.'

Variety is the spice of life, especially when it comes to cooking. That's why I love recipes like meat loaf that allow countless variations, taking its taste to new horizons.

19 MEAT LOAF

Beef, like chicken, provides all the amino acids we need to synthesize neurotransmitters. It delivers proteins with B vitamins and iron that our bodies can absorb easily. Unfortunately, we cannot gauge the quality of the meat that we buy. Commercial meat tends to be polluted by antibiotics and hormones. If you can, buy organic meat.

Enjoying meat once in a while outweighs for me the threat of pollutants. Our bodies are designed to consume all kinds of food, but I try to combine meat with as many healthy ingredients as possible. Parsley, garlic and onions provide a lot of antioxidants. I also serve meaty dishes with salad as a side dish. Although I have given a recipe here, I keep experimenting with meat loaf and I urge you to do the same.

VARIATIONS

- Imbibe Indian flavours with garam masala, ground ginger, chopped fresh coriander and chillies.
- Fill the meat loaf with a mixture of spinach, mushrooms and garlic. Chop the vegetables finely; spread half the minced meat in your baking dish. Cover it with the vegetables and the rest of the minced meat.
- Top the meat loaf with a cup of grated cheese and give it five minutes under the grill.

INGREDIENTS

(Serves 4-6)

- 1 kg minced beef
- 3 cups rolled oats
- 4 cloves garlic
- 2 big onions
- 1 cup parsley (or any other herb you like)
- 4 eggs
- 3 tbsp olive oil
- Salt
- Pepper

METHOD

Crush garlic. Wash parsley, clean onions and chop finely.

Place minced meat into a bowl. Add eggs, oats and vegetables, about two teaspoons of salt and pepper and combine.

Spread two tablespoons olive oil over bottom of an ovenproof dish. Form meat mixture into loaf. Place into dish. Spread remaining olive oil over loaf. That helps to form a nice crust. Bake for one hour at 200 degrees Celsius.

SWEET LULL OF ENDORPHINS

When a mental disease holds you in its grip, you tend to perceive your surroundings as weird. While suffering from anorexia nervosa, I considered the appetite of my father and brothers unhealthy. The rebels celebrated Saturday mornings with an opulent brunch. Fresh bread-rolls were served with a variety of cold cuts. The table was decked out in Bone China porcelain over antique cross-stitched linen. I limited my intake to a single bread roll while everybody dug in.

This happened during the seventies when as skinny as possible was the beauty ideal of the European woman. I became super skinny for the sake of beauty – and completely obsessed. You had to control your body 24/7 to avoid giving in to your appetite. You had to count the calories of every morsel that you put into your mouth. How else could you keep a weight of forty-nine kilograms being 175 centimetres tall?

During this time, I met my first boyfriend at high school. I had found a victim willing to supply all the affection I had missed from my parents. For the first time, I was in control of a relationship and I abused my power to the fullest – without malice. I had no idea how much I was exploiting the guy. Many times, I staged tearful fights because somehow it felt so good. Of course my boyfriend was always the guilty one.

I guess I had found a way to enjoy endorphins, our bodies' own opiates. Endorphins were discovered only in 1973. They ease feelings of pain during shock, stress or trauma. Serious exercise releases endorphins; tears also make endorphins work in our brains. That explains why some people get stuck in painful relationships, keep playing the drama queen or inflict pain on their bodies. The endorphin rush may be the main reason why so many teenage girls cut themselves nowadays.

We don't have to hurt to produce endorphins. Music, dancing, singing, a workout, aromas like vanilla or lavender, chocolate, spicy food, sex and laughter stimulate the release of endorphins. Unfortunately, habituation kicks in quickly. That's why it is so important to change things. Remember, a joke gets old very quickly. In our modern world we face colossal problems and a single person can do little about big issues.

Frittata is a great way of dishing up a tasty and healthy meal in no time at all.

20 RAINBOW FRITTATA

The French omelette is cooked only on one side, while the Italian frittata is flipped or finished under the grill. Anything goes with a frittata. You can use every kind of vegetables, herbs, cheese, fish, or meat. I like to top it off with grated cheese that turns into a lovely crust.

Only one ingredient remains the same: eggs. I call the recipe rainbow frittata, because I use as many different coloured vegetables as possible. Eggs and cheese provide the amino acids for neurotransmitters, and the vegetables provide the vitamins and minerals to synthesize them.

INGREDIENTS

(Serves 4)

- 6 eggs
- 1 big carrot
- 1 medium beetroot
- 1 bundle spring onions
- 2 cloves garlic
- 1 bundle parsley
- 3 tbsp olive oil
- 100 gm grated cheese
- Salt
- Pepper

METHOD

Clean and chop spring onions. Crush garlic. Peel and grate carrot and beetroot. Wash parsley and chop it.

Heat oil in a non-stick pan. Fry spring onions, carrot and beetroot over low fire until soft, around three to four minutes. Crack eggs into a bowl and season with salt and pepper.

Add parsley and garlic to vegetables and fry for another minute. Spread egg mixture over vegetables and cover pan with a lid.

When eggs have set, cover frittata with grated cheese. Grill until the cheese has formed a lovely crust.

EGG-CEPTIONAL QUALITIES

Eggs not only provide a good dose of low cost protein, they also contain plenty of choline. Without choline our bodies cannot absorb folic acid, and it is essential for methylation, the important transport cycle in our bodies. Choline is also an important building block for neurotransmitters. Egg yolks are the richest known source for choline. Nowadays experts say everybody can eat one or two eggs a day. They are also a prime source for carotenoids and B vitamins.

OXYTOCIN

Oxytocin, also called cuddle or trust hormone, acts as a neurotransmitter in the brain. Although oxytocin was already discovered in 1906, we have learnt about its role in social relations only within the last decade. Its name means 'quick birth'. During birth, high levels of oxytocin make the uterus contract and bring on lactation.

Oxytocin induces feelings of optimism, increases self-esteem and builds trust. This hormone also plays a part in sexual arousal and orgasms. But we don't need to become intimate to make oxytocin work for us. Oxytocin is stimulated by many social activities like hugging a friend or stroking a pet.

21 FRENCH-STYLE OMELETTE

Julia Child hits the spot when she calls an omelette 'a smooth, gently swelling, golden oval that is tender and creamy inside'.

That distinguishes it from a frittata where the eggs envelop a variety of ingredients. Julia Child recommends practising omelettes, 'willing to throw some away'. I am not a genius in the kitchen, but I beg to differ. Making an omelette is easy; you just have to know how and be ready to make some noise. The result is a wonderfully fluffy omelette, done in an astonishingly short amount of time.

INGREDIENTS

(Makes 1)

- 2 tbsp butter
- 2 or 3 eggs
- Salt
- Pepper

METHOD

You need a non-stick pan with sloping sides.

Use enough butter. You need high heat so that eggs coagulate immediately. While butter melts in pan, crack eggs into a bowl, add salt and pepper and blend with a fork.

Swirl butter so it coats bottom and sides of pan. Place eggs into pan and start shaking vigorously back and forth in one direction. Constant shaking loosens the eggs from the sides and forms an omelette. Serve hot.

CREATE COSY MOMENTS

Touching and cuddling was not part of our family life. As

a teenager, I was starved for food and skin contact. My first boyfriend remedied this lack. We cuddled and kissed for hours. Sex did not attract me at all. I had too much to do with counting calories and controlling my desires for chocolate cake. My boyfriend also came from a Catholic family; premarital sex was still considered taboo.

There is nothing wrong with living alone but we all need social interaction. Any kind of physical contact releases the happy-maker oxytocin, so touch the people you meet. Shake their hand, hug them or tip them on the shoulder. Even gazing at someone or thinking in a positive way about a person does the trick.

If you feel too vulnerable with humans, start with pets or digital friends. Every time you feel good after interacting, tell yourself, 'I have created this feeling'. The goal is not to trust or bond with anybody. You don't want to become the victim of a con artist.

When you want to improve social contacts, it helps to remember that you have to be trustworthy to trust. We tend to project our own mistakes onto the persons we meet. Make it a point to keep promises. Don't commit if you are not sure you can follow through. Enjoy the good feeling when you keep a promise.

The following recipe warms my heart because it comes straight from my mother's kitchen. My mother called this dish Russian eggs, what is otherwise known as devilled eggs or stuffed eggs. These dishes follow one main thread. You boil the eggs, halve them, remove the egg yolks, mix them with ingredients and fill this blend into the halves.

22 RUSSIAN EGGS

Most devilled eggs feature a bit of mayonnaise. I never buy mayonnaise and I don't like to keep it for long. I want my recipes to be fast and easy. That's why I avoid mayonnaise. My mother used generous amounts of butter and anchovies. Both my men love these Russian eggs.

INGREDIENTS

(Makes 4)

- 8 eggs
- 6 tbsp butter
- 1 tin of anchovies (2 ounces or 55 gm)
- Salt
- Pepper

METHOD

Place eggs into a pot, cover with water and boil for ten minutes. Prepare ice water in a bowl. Transfer eggs from boiling into ice water. The temperature shock ensures easy peeling.

Peel eggs and halve them. Place yolks into a bowl, add butter, anchovies, salt and pepper. Combine well. Adjust seasoning and fill egg halves.

EAT MORE ANCHOVIES

Experts recommend eating small fish like anchovies to counteract overfishing. Small fishes could not only feed the three major tropical tuna species which land on our plates, they could also feed us. Fishing boats catch thousands of tons of anchovies every year. Most are ground into fishmeal and shipped around the world to feed chickens, pigs and farmed fish. This is a huge waste, not to mention the pollution and the fuel consumed for the transport.

SEROTONIN AND SOCIAL STATUS

Serotonin is another hormone acting as a neurotransmitter. It was discovered in 1948 as a substance that constricts blood vessels, hence its name, meaning serum that gives tone. Eighty per cent of our body's serotonin regulates the gut's movements. In the brain, serotonin calms and induces feelings of contentment. Low levels of serotonin are involved in many disorders like depression, anxiety and obsessive-compulsive disorder.

23 QUINOA SPINACH-MUSHROOM PIE

Quinoa is the only plant that provides all nine amino acids essential for human beings. High protein foods such as meat, eggs and beef contain more than twenty different amino acids. Beans and grains contain fewer amino acids. That's why vegetarians need to know how to combine foods to get complete proteins. This recipe works well with brown rice, millet or grains of wheat or rye. Just replace the quinoa with equal amounts of these grains.

QUINOA, INCAN 'GOLD'

In 300 BC, quinoa was a staple of the people living in the Andes mountains of South America. Scientists call quinoa a pseudo cereal, because it looks and is used like a grain, but is in fact a seed.

Quinoa contains all nine essential amino acids and more healthy fats than cereals, even small amounts of omega-3 fatty acids. It provides plenty of calcium, magnesium, manganese, copper and iron. Quinoa also contains amazing amounts of phytonutrients. It has more quercetin and kaempferol than high-flavonoid berries like cranberry or lingonberry.

INGREDIENTS

(Serves 8)

- 2 cups quinoa
- 3 packets (600 gm) fresh mushrooms, any type you like
- 3 big bundles (600 gm) spinach leaves
- 3 big leeks, around 500 gm together
- 5 sprigs fresh thyme
- 4 eggs
- 8 tbsp olive oil
- 20 gm sesame seeds
- 4 cups liquid
- Salt
- Pepper

METHOD

Wash and chop vegetables and mushrooms. Put two tablespoons olive oil in a pan and fry leeks until translucent. Add thyme and mushrooms and fry for ten minutes. Finally add spinach and cook until wilted. Season with salt and pepper.

Wash quinoa until water remains clear. Put two tablespoons olive oil in a pot, and roast quinoa golden brown. Add four cups of liquid and a teaspoon of salt. The liquid can be water, vegetable broth or excess liquid from the spinach-mushroom mix. Cook until quinoa has soaked up all liquid; it should take around fifteen minutes. Let it cool down, and combine with eggs.

Spread remaining four tablespoons of olive oil over bottom of a big pie dish. I have one with a diameter of 29 centimetres (12.5 inches), perfect for this dish. Distribute about one-third of the cooked quinoa over bottom of dish. Mix rest of quinoa with vegetables and spread in dish. Sprinkle sesame seeds over top. Bake at 190 degrees Celsius for twenty-five minutes. The sesame should turn golden brown.

BE PROUD OF WHAT YOU DO

I write cookbooks, manage a website, and write a newsletter every month. I constantly research food trends and experiment in my kitchen. That keeps me on my toes.

Our brain compares us to our peers all the time. Of course I would love to be as popular as Jamie Oliver but the leader of the pack is always under scrutiny. When you do your best, you can be proud. Pat yourself on the shoulder and accept who you are.

We need to combine proteins: nuts with whole wheat deliver all nine amino acids for body and brain.

24 WHOLE WHEAT PASTA WITH WALNUT SAUCE

Like pesto you can buy walnut sauce in every Italian supermarket but it is difficult to find a recipe. Italian cooking enhances the taste of the main ingredient with less spices. That does not mean it tastes bland but seasoning with salt and pepper is important.

I discovered this recipe in Milano. Walnuts with dairy and whole wheat provide proteins and vitamin B for neurotransmitters.

INGREDIENTS

(Serves 4)

- 100 gm walnuts
- 5 tbsp olive oil
- Salt
- Pepper
- 1 packet (200 ml) cream
- 1 packet (500 gm) whole wheat pasta
- Grated parmigiano or grana cheese to serve with the pasta

METHOD

You need a blender for this recipe. Chop walnuts, then add chunks of cheese, olive oil and cream. Blend together. Season with salt and pepper. For zest, add ground red chillies. The walnut sauce should have a thick, creamy consistency.

Bring a big pot of water to boil. Add two tablespoons of salt and the pasta. Cook according to the directions on the packet. Stir six tablespoons of pasta water into the sauce. This makes it easier to coat the pasta. Drain pasta, mix with walnut sauce and serve immediately with plenty of grated parmigiano or grana cheese.

WALNUTS, NUTRITIONAL POWERHOUSE

The walnut is a nutritional powerhouse, a rich source of omega-3 fatty acids, copper, manganese, magnesium and vitamin E and several B vitamins. Like other tree nuts, it contains a lot of protein and fibre as well. Experts recommend eating the skin of walnuts, because it contains many flavonoids, tannins and phenolic acids.

HEALTHY HAPPY-MAKERS

When trying to increase neurotransmitters in your brain remember to balance it. Don't focus on one – try to improve all four. The following recipe completes my section on building blocks for the brain. The second vegetarian combination for complete proteins is legumes with whole grains.

25 MEXICAN BEANS AND BROWN RICE

In English they are called kidney or pinto beans, in Hindi they are called rajma. This recipe is inspired by Mexican cuisine. In India, rajma are typically served in a Punjabi curry style or dal. This recipe delivers a dish that is a lot lighter and a lot faster to cook.

INGREDIENTS

(Serves 4)

- 1½ cups dry rajma beans
- 1 cup brown rice
- 1 packet tomato puree (200 ml)
- 2 carrots
- 2 beetroots
- 1 small stalk celery
- 3 onions
- 5 cloves garlic
- 3 bay leaves
- 3 big red fresh chillies
- 6 tbsp extra virgin olive oil
- 4 cups vegetable stock
- Salt
- Pepper
- 1 green bell pepper
- 1 cup fresh coriander
- 200 gm cheese

METHOD

Soak rajma beans overnight in water. Rinse and place in a pressure cooker. Clean carrots, beetroots, celery, onions, garlic and chillies. Chop vegetables finely in a blender.

Add vegetables and bay leaves to pressure cooker. Wash rice and add with two tablespoons olive oil, salt and pepper, and four cups vegetable stock or water. Close lid and cook for forty-five minutes on a low flame after first whistle.

Wash green bell pepper and coriander and chop finely. Grate cheese.

After cooking, add rest of the olive oil. I do this to preserve the nutrition of the olive oil. You can replace oil with butter or ghee. Serve rice topped with chopped bell peppers, fresh coriander and grated cheese.

FIND YOUR VOCATION

I believe everybody has hidden talents. You need to find yours and how you can express them in the best possible way. I consider myself a good cook but I have never dreamed of having a restaurant. It would completely destroy my pleasure in concocting tasty food.

Instead of running a restaurant, writing cookbooks works well for me. I learn about ingredients and develop new recipes. That stimulates dopamine and oxytocin. Endorphins happen naturally along the way because I love cooking with music. Burns and cuts occur quite frequently too.

Publishing books is great for serotonin levels. My first two cookbooks have won the Gourmand World Cookbook

Awards, another serotonin source. While writing, I reap dopamine with every step. I pat myself on the shoulder and hear my internal cheerleaders applaud.

However, without enough amino acids floating around in the blood stream, my happy-making circuit could not work. We need a protein-rich diet to keep up a steady supply of neurotransmitters, the important happy-makers in our brain.

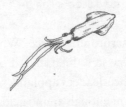

CHAPTER 3

OMEGA-3 SOURCES

Another essential component of a happy-making diet is omega-3. Humans have known about the importance of fish oil for thousands of years. Ancient Greeks and Romans rubbed fish oil on their skin and ingested it as medicine. Fishermen along the coasts of Northern Europe valued oil from cod livers for centuries as cure for all.

I don't even want to imagine how this oil tasted. It was made by cutting fish livers along with the gall bladders, throwing them into barrels and letting them rot. Pharmacists of this period described it as an abomination. In 1841, an Edinburgh physician published a treatise on cod liver oil after he had spent some years in Germany and observed the treatment of various diseases. This treatise arose interest on both sides of the Atlantic and by mid-century a large cod liver oil industry was thriving in New England.

The popularity of cod liver oil was based on its reputation to cure 'consumption', a leading cause of death in the 19th century. A number of diseases like tuberculosis, rheumatism, and rickets were called consumption. Although Robert Koch discovered the bacillus that causes tuberculosis in 1882, in the public eye cod liver oil remained the main medicine for this disease for a long time.

Nowadays, fish oil supplements and neutral-tasting gelatine capsules are popular, but for other reasons. We know a lot more about the immense importance of omega-3 fatty acids. Scientists started investigating their significance in the 1930s. In 1980 a study about non-existent coronary heart disease among Eskimos put omega-3 fatty acids on the list of essential nutrients.

Andrew Stoll points out in his book *The Omega-3 Connection* that since 1945, US Americans have eaten constantly less omega-3 and more seed oils. At the same time, depression has increased twentyfold.

It is difficult to prove a connection. After looking through many sources – and eating fish regularly for years – I think we benefit greatly from this substance. Omega-3 fatty acids not only reduce inflammation, they improve our mood by facilitating chemical processes in our brains. How omega-3 exactly affects the brain is still unknown. One reason could be its flexibility. Membranes made from fat encase our neurons. The easier these membranes move, the better they transport information.

THE FEEL-GOOD FAT

Countries with diets rich in fish, for example Japan, show low levels of depression. Omega-3 fatty acids not only make you feel good, they also boost brainpower in children, prevent disorders like Attention Deficit Hyperactivity Disorder

(ADHD), dementia and Alzheimer's. The American Heart Association recommends omega-3 fatty acids to avoid heart disease. Low levels of omega-3 have been linked with bipolar disorder, schizophrenia, autism and Alzheimer's disease.

During my stint with anorexia, I started collecting cookbooks. I wanted to introduce more fish recipes because seafood is low in calories. Sadly, cookbooks can restrict one's creativity in the kitchen. One gave me the impression that you cannot prepare a bouillabaisse if you are not born in France. I had tasted this fish soup in a small lane surrounding the harbour of Marseille and it did not strike me as overly complicated. Still, I did not dare to cook it as a teenager and stuck to simpler recipes.

Fish soup requires time and effort, but the result is well worth it. You can prepare a big pot and then freeze portions. Just bring the base for the soup to a boil and throw in the fish and other seafood, which cooks in a few minutes.

26 FISH SOUP

You need fish bones for the fish stock, which is a must for the soup. Buy any fatty fish like snapper or rockfish. Get it filleted and take home the bones and the head of the fish. Fat carries the flavours of our food. Don't use tuna or kingfish for the stock. When using a flatfish like pomfret, don't simmer the stock longer than twenty minutes.

You can add any seafood to the soup. You need around two kilograms of seafood (before cleaning) for four generous servings. Always serve this soup with a lot of baguette.

INGREDIENTS FOR SOUP

(Serves 12)

- Bones and head of a fish that weighs around 1.5 kg
- 1 kg red tomatoes
- 1 tin (400 gm) peeled Italian tomatoes
- 3 stalks celery
- ½ kg onions
- 4 big carrots
- 10 cloves garlic
- 1 bundle parsley
- 1 tbsp peppercorns
- 3 bay leaves
- 10 tbsp olive oil
- Salt
- Pepper

SEAFOOD

(Serves 4)

- 500 gm fish fillet
- 500 gm cleaned prawns
- 500 gm squids
- 500 gm mussels (with the shell)

METHOD

Heat three tablespoons olive oil in a pot; brown fish bones and fish head. You need to see caramelisation on bottom of pot. Add three litres of water; add peppercorns, bay leaves, one carrot and one onion, roughly chopped. Bring to a boil and simmer for one hour or more. If you have large squids, you might want to clean and boil them in this fish stock until tender. Drain stock through a finely meshed sieve.

Immerse tomatoes in boiling water, peel and remove seeds. Chop vegetables and place with garlic into a pot. Cover with fish stock, add olive oil and simmer for one hour. If you like it spicy, add three red chillies. Season with salt and pepper.

After cooling, puree vegetables with a blender stick. Season with pepper and salt. Divide fish soup into portions. Keep what you want to serve immediately and freeze the rest.

Bring fish soup to a boil and add seafood according to cooking time. Fish fillet needs five minutes, squid ten minutes and prawns one minute. If you want to add mussels, wash well, put into a pan and fry over medium heat. Add all opened mussels to fish soup and boil for two minutes.

SHARP MIND? THANK SQUIDS

The flesh of squids provides a lot of nutrients. Squids have a lot of protein, a few carbohydrates and a little fat. What makes them so precious is the kind of fat they provide: a specific fatty acid found only in fish oil, docosahexaenoic acid, or DHA. 100 grams of squid contain 0.38 grams of DHA and only 78 calories. Furthermore, squids provide selenium, phosphorus, riboflavin and vitamin B for a sharp mind.

EAT MORE SEAFOOD

Today, taste is not an issue with fish oil any more. Fish oil supplements deliver omega-3 fatty acids in neutral-tasting capsules. However, I believe the best way to ingest the feel-good fat is by eating plenty of seafood.

During my quest to feed seafood to my men without adding hours to my kitchen duties, I once served a whole fish, baked in the oven. Just slice the fish open on the sides, stuff the belly with some herbs, season the skin and cook it at lowest heat until it is done.

27 FISH WITH BEURRE BLANC

Although the fish turns succulent and flaky with this recipe, you need sauce with it. I chose Beurre Blanc, a classic French butter sauce – delicious, yet quick and easy. 100 years ago, a French woman invented this sauce. Clémence Lefeuvre served it at her restaurant 'La Buvette de la Marine' on the banks of the Loire River.

Some people add cream to Beurre Blanc. I stick with the classic recipe that uses butter only. I never failed with this sauce. The only thing to remember is to cut the butter into small pieces, keep it in the fridge until needed and whisk it slowly into the sauce.

INGREDIENTS

(Serves 4)

- 1 fish of around 1.5 kg
- 1 handful fresh thyme
- 4 tbsp olive oil
- 3 cloves garlic

- Salt
- Pepper

FOR BEURRE BLANC

- ¼ cup white wine
- ¼ cup white wine vinegar
- 2 purple shallots (or any kind of onion)
- 6 peppercorns
- 200 gm butter
- 2 tbsp lemon juice
- Salt
- Ground white pepper

METHOD

When you buy fish, ask the vendor to clean insides and flake skin. At home, rinse it well. Cut diagonally three times through both sides of fish. Slice garlic and push some slices into cuts. Rub salt and pepper over skin and stuff belly with thyme and rest of garlic.

Spread olive oil over a cookie sheet and bake at lowest heat in the oven. A 1.5 kilograms fish takes around forty-five minutes. You should not see any pink when you carefully check the flesh at its thickest place with a knife or fork.

For Beurre Blanc place white wine, vinegar and finely chopped shallots with peppercorns into a saucepan. Reduce over high heat to three tablespoons liquid. Cut butter into small cubes and keep cold.

Strain reduction through a sieve; place into a saucepan

over low heat. Whisk all butter cubes slowly into reduction. Switch off heat and add lemon juice. Season with salt and pepper and serve immediately.

You can take the fish whole to the table and dissect it there or you can clean it in the kitchen and serve only the flesh.

MEDITERRANEAN HAPPINESS

In Greece I discovered my first husband and my love for seafood. In 1984, I arrived at the island Folegandros for holiday from my work at the newspaper. The blue Aegean Sea separates this tiny island from its famous neighbour Santorini. Travel guides call it an island of bewitching beauty – weather-beaten rocks covered with olive and pine trees. You had to climb several kilometres down a valley to reach the beach Agios Nikolaos. There I met a student from Athens with long, brown locks. He looked like a Greek god.

One evening, he took me out to a small eatery on the next beach. A couple of fishermen were celebrating a catch of lobsters. The best ones were thrown into boiling water, cleaned and served to the few guests with generous amounts of ouzo, Greek liquor flavoured with anis. To demonstrate their jolly mood, they thrashed plates with gusto on the floor. 'Hopa,' they shouted and bang went the next plate. I watched with fascination. My love explained that in Greece you smash plates to show happiness.

Never again have I eaten such fresh and tasty lobster. It was dressed simply with lemon juice and olive oil. Greece was the place where I left all my figure problems behind. After I had finished my apprenticeship at the newspaper with the journalist diploma, I left Bavaria and joined my first husband in Athens.

I had no idea how we would feed ourselves. I just followed my heart. In Greece, I was completely lost. I did not understand the language and spent countless hours listening to my future husband and his friends chatting away. We lived at his parents' house so we did not spend a lot of money.

I discovered the Greek kitchen during the two years I stayed in the country, especially seafood. Athens has the most delightful fish market. I often took the subway from our suburban home and got calamari, prawns or mackerels. We grilled the seafood over charcoals in the courtyard, basting them with sticks of rosemary cut from the garden, dipped into olive oil and mixed with lemon juice.

The following recipe delivers a complete seafood meal in a packet. Although the technique in this recipe could be called 'en papillote', I prefer the Italian name, 'in cartoccio'. This dish offers dinner with little effort. Best of all, your plates remain almost clean. This is also a great recipe for a festive dinner with friends.

28 FISH IN CARTOCCIO

Cooking in 'cartoccio' is a great way of preparing foods that cook quickly. My choice of ingredients is only a suggestion. A bed of vegetables prevents the fish from burning while the moisture of the vegetables steams the fish in the parcel. This is especially important in a gas oven where the heat comes only from below.

INGREDIENTS

(Serves 4)

- 🌱 4 fish fillets (around 800 gm total)
- 🌱 1 lemon
- 🌱 2 big leeks
- 🌱 1 medium zucchini
- 🌱 150 gm rucola
- 🌱 Chives
- 🌱 4 cloves garlic
- 🌱 4 tbsp olive oil
- 🌱 Salt
- 🌱 Pepper
- 🌱 Parchment paper
- 🌱 Aluminium foil

METHOD

Wash fish fillets. Preheat oven to 210 degrees Celsius. Fold parchment paper and cut four heart shapes, big enough to hold fish filets and vegetables.

Crush garlic. Clean leeks, zucchini and chives and slice finely. Wash rucola and cut into one inch wide strips.

Assemble parcels. Open paper-hearts and distribute leeks evenly over one half. Cover with zucchini slices. Sprinkle salt and pepper over vegetables.

Place fish fillets on top of vegetables. If fish fillets are thin and big, halve and layer them. Drizzle lemon juice, salt and pepper over fillets. Top fish with crushed garlic, rucola and chives. Season with salt and pepper and drizzle with olive oil.

Fold paper over the fish and tuck borders together, starting by blunt end. Twist the tip to seal packet. Place paper parcel on aluminium foil and fold together tightly.

Bake for twenty minutes. Let it rest for five minutes before serving.

LEEKS, OVERLOOKED VEGETABLE

This vegetable tends to be overshadowed by onions, garlic, shallots and spring onions. They belong to the Allium family, a kind of lily. I like to use leeks because they cook faster than onions and have a sweeter flavour.

Leeks contain the flavonoid kaempferol, which protects blood vessels from damages by relaxing them. A lot of folate makes leeks a cardio-protective food. Antioxidant polyphenols are great for blood vessels too. Leeks also contain plenty of manganese, iron, vitamin C and B6.

DECISION TO BECOME A MOTHER

Love without financial base hardly ever lasts. After two years in Greece, we had spent all my savings but not managed to find a way to feed ourselves. My husband liked to call himself a 'misfit in society'. When the Greek army called him to serve his duty, we got married and moved to Germany. I supported his decision not to touch a gun.

In Germany, I worked again as a journalist and convinced my husband to learn a profession because he had left university without a degree. He chose to become a gardener. I did not mind to be the breadwinner. Unconsciously I feared control. On the surface, my husband seemed like the complete opposite of my father. Yet, in all our fights I somehow got the feeling of not being good enough, of being focused too much on material well-being. Our relationship dragged along.

I reached my 30th birthday, a turning point: I woke up in the morning and knew that I wanted a child. 'Good, I stay home and you keep working,' was my husband's reply. But I wanted to have time for my baby, not juggle a career and motherhood. This was the last drop and I asked for divorce.

When I met the man of my life thanks to the Enfield Bullet, I made one thing clear: I wanted to raise a child and I did not want to work. For good measure, I also threw in that I didn't cook. I did not want a man that needed to be serviced by his wife. We got married in Milano. Both our families were happy that we settled down. Soon after, I became pregnant, one of the happiest times of my life.

We lived in a beautiful house in Goa. I did not even suffer from morning sickness. We went to the beach every day. After swimming, we had lunch at a place known for fresh fish. I am sure that I ate enough omega-3 during my pregnancy. My son turned out super intelligent. Omega-3 plays a vital role in the mother's womb for the development of the baby's brain.

Breastfed babies receive more of this vital fat than bottle-raised ones because infant formula is not required to contain omega-3. My son was born in 1999 under the sign of Cancer and – like my husband – he loves to eat crabs. That's why I learnt how to prepare them. I still recall the first crab I bought. When my son was small, he loved fish markets to look at seafood, a bit like a visit to the zoo. One day, we discovered a big crab and he insisted on taking it home. He played with it the entire afternoon. Then I threw the poor thing into a big pot with boiling water, cleaned it and served it Greek style with lemon-olive oil dressing.

29 JUMBO CRABS ASIAN STYLE

My men prefer crabs Asian style. After freezing and scrubbing the crabs, I cut them into pieces and steam them on a bed of Thai bean noodles. While the crabs are steaming, I prepare the sauce in a wok and toss the crab in it before serving it with the noodles.

If your family likes rice, you might want to serve these crabs with double the amount of sauce and steamed rice. It is difficult to provide amounts of ingredients for this recipe. You need around one kilogram big crab per person. You can use normal sized crabs for this dish but they don't deliver the same degree of satisfaction.

The sauce depends on your taste. Just cook away and season until it tastes right.

INGREDIENTS

(Serves 4)

- 4 big crabs
- 100 gm Thai bean threads
- 2 bundles spring onions
- 6 garlic cloves

- 🌶 1 piece of fresh ginger, around 5 cm long
- 🌶 6 small red Thai chillies (or other chillies)
- 🌶 4 tbsp olive oil
- 🌶 3 tbsp soya sauce
- 🌶 2 tbsp oyster sauce
- 🌶 1 tbsp fish sauce
- 🌶 1 tbsp sugar
- 🌶 ½ cup white wine
- 🌶 ½ cup water

METHOD

Put crabs into freezer so they won't feel pain when you chop them. Rinse well under running water and scrub with a brush.

Place crab belly up onto a chopping board. Pull away small triangular bit of shell and stick a knife through crab. This kills it. Then stick your fingers into hole and pull off shell. Remove feathery gills and yellow 'butter'. Chop crab into half. Break off legs and claws, and crack shells with a hammer or meat tenderiser. Soften bean threads in a bowl of warm water.

Place a steamer inset into a big pot and cover bottom with hot water. Spread bean threads over inset, then pile crab pieces on top. Close with a lid and steam for fifteen to twenty minutes. All shells should turn orange.

Clean and chop spring onions, garlic, chillies and ginger. Heat oil in a wok, fry onions, garlic and ginger, add sauces and sugar and adjust seasoning. Toss steamed crabs in sauce.

ALL THE GOODNESS OF SEAFOOD

Crabs are appreciated all over the world because they taste delicious. Crab meat delivers all the qualities of other seafood. They contain a lot of calcium, copper, zinc, phosphorus, iron and plenty of omega-3. They also provide chromium, a chemical element that helps insulin to metabolise sugar and lowers blood glucose levels. Another element from the periodic table that crabs deliver in a form fit for humans is selenium, a powerful antioxidant.

SHARED EXPERIENCES SOLVE MYSTERIES

Omega-3 enables faster communication inside the brain and raises dopamine and serotonin levels. Both neurotransmitter levels are connected. When you do something good for either of them, it also affects the other one. How this works remains a mystery so far. We all keep learning.

Returning from Greece, I had to start my professional life from scratch. I had idled away two years of my life. Although these years had been great and I had learned to speak Greek but the German newspaper editors were not impressed. After slaving as a freelancer for one year, I was properly employed again as an editor in Regensburg, the hometown of my parents.

Regensburg is my favourite place in Germany, with its medieval centre around a gothic cathedral at the banks of the river Danube. The university attracts young people and furthers the cultural scene. Big factories make it a booming city. I was happy in Regensburg but occasionally I felt empty. There had to be more to life than pursuing a career. I participated in soul-searching workshops.

During one of these workshops I commented how my father had terrified me and how my parents had controlled my life. A friend remarked, 'Your husband does the same in a different way. He always says he is free of material desires. When he finally does want something, you immediately fulfil his wish. Two weeks ago you cancelled our girls' night-out because he wanted to see a movie.'

I felt like a blind person who could suddenly see. I had always done exactly what my husband wanted. I had moved to Greece. I had returned to Germany and financed our life. He had learned a profession but he considered it beneath him to work.

Sometimes we are so enmeshed in relationships that we lose ourselves. A simple comment can cut through illusions. 'Simple is best' applies to many occasions in life. It is especially true when it comes to cooking Italian. Italians never compromise with quality of produce.

30 MUSSELS ALLA MARINARA

When you want to make mussels the Italian way, you need first class olive oil and absolutely fresh mussels. The mussels should be alive when you buy them and their shells should be shut firmly. You also need a really big pan with a tight fitting lid, if possible, a glass one.

An Italian marquesa taught me this recipe many years ago in the kitchen of her mansion in Matera, south Italy. Through the window we could see rocky hills mingling with fields of golden wheat. This landscape has served as the backdrop for many Spaghetti Westerns in the 1960s. Clint Eastwood started his career there.

I like this recipe so much that I never thought about changing it. The sauce requires dry white wine and plenty of parsley. Serve the mussels with baguette to mop up the sauce.

The mussels cook quickly. The biggest amount of work is the cleaning. To be sure that they don't harbour any sand, soak them for one hour in salted, cold water. They will expel any sand during this soaking time. You can serve mussels as a starter to a festive meal.

INGREDIENTS

(Serves 4)

- 2 kg big, black mussels or any other kind that you find (as a starter 1.5 kg might be enough)
- 4 big cloves of garlic
- 5 tbsp extra virgin olive oil
- 1 bundle of flat leaf parsley
- ¼ cup (50 ml) white wine
- Salt
- Pepper

METHOD

Brush mussels and remove beard, the spongy bit hanging out. Soak in cold salt water for one hour. Wash and finely chop parsley.

Heat the olive oil in a pan and fry garlic. If you like zest, add fresh, chopped chillies. Add mussels and white wine. Close with a lid. In a few minutes mussels should open. Stir well. Cook for two minutes after shells have opened.

Season with pepper and salt and stir chopped parsley into sauce. Serve immediately.

MUSSELS BOOST SWIMMERS

Like all other seafood, mussels contain a wealth of nutrition. They deliver vitamin A, B12, other B vitamins and lots of precious omega-3.

They also provide plenty of the essential mineral selenium. One class of enzymes in the human body, the so-called 'selenoproteins', need selenium to function. These enzymes support the work of muscles in the human body, balance the levels of thyroid hormones and support sperm production in men. Maybe that's why oysters are supposed to be an aphrodisiac?

OMEGA-3 FROM ANIMALS

Eating food with a lot of omega-3 two to three times a week keeps the blues at bay. If you are concerned about heavy metals in fish, stick to small varieties like sardines and anchovies. Heavy metals accumulate in predators, not in small fish feeding on algae and phytoplankton.

If you want to reap the full benefits of omega-3 fatty acids, go for animal sources. You cannot get the same effect from omega-3 fatty acids from plants because the human body can hardly transform it into the kinds of omega-3 we need, the eicosapentaenoic acid (EPA) and docosahexaenoic acid (DHA). Meat delivers a lot of omega-3 if it comes from grass-fed animals, as does seafood.

The following recipe uses tinned tuna, an easy solution to serve seafood. Considering that almost every food item, even organic produce, contains pollution, I think it is safe to eat tuna from a can once in a while.

Several kinds end up in tins that we purchase from markets. Its place high in the food chain makes it accumulate pollution from its prey, especially the heavy metal mercury. The highest levels of mercury are found in albacore tuna, called 'solid white' on tins. Dark coloured tuna from smaller species have lower levels of mercury. This tuna is called 'chunk light'.

Health organisations recommend that pregnant women and small children don't eat tuna. Mercury hinders the development of the brain. However, many experts think that the benefits of tuna outweigh the health risk. This fish is an excellent source of minerals like magnesium, potassium and selenium. It also provides complex B vitamins and omega-3 fatty acids.

31 OATS AND TUNA BURGERS

Opt for tuna packed in brine, not oil. Omega-3 fatty acids leach into the oil. When you drain the tuna, you throw away some of the good stuff. These fish burgers are loaded with fibres and minerals thanks to the big amount of oats.

INGREDIENTS

(Makes 4)

- 1 tin tuna in brine
- 2 bundles spring onions
- 2 eggs
- 1 cup oats
- 5 tbsp olive oil
- Salt
- Pepper
- Bread crumbs
- Burger buns

METHOD

Clean spring onions and chop finely in a blender. Add drained tuna and blend again.

Place tuna into a bowl; add eggs, oats, two tablespoons olive oil, salt and pepper and mix. If eggs are small you might need to add one more. Form patties.

Put breadcrumbs into a plate and coat the patties.

Heat olive oil in a non-stick pan and fry them for 5 minutes on each side until golden brown.

Place the patty inside the burger bun and enjoy!

SURPRISING END TO LIFE IN LIMBO

At thirty, I had reached a crossroad in my life but I did not know what to do. My biological clock was ticking loudly. During holidays in Goa I rode a bike for the first time: wind in my hair, palm trees flying by, freedom. On the last evening of the holidays I watched the sunset and listened to some people talking about buying an Enfield. 'How much do you have to pay for a big bike like that?' I heard myself asking. 1,000 dollars! All of a sudden, I knew what to do. I would buy an Enfield and drive through India while figuring out the direction of my life.

It took me two years to finalize my divorce and prepare for the trip, time in limbo for more soul searching. I even became vegetarian but I was never convinced. It is much more difficult to feed your body properly. This applies especially to omega-3.

Some people recommend flaxseeds and walnuts as sources for omega-3 fatty acids. Human bodies are only able to convert less than 5 per cent of plant omega-3 into the fatty acids our bodies can use. Soybeans and canola are also hailed as omega-3 sources but I do not recommend these genetically modified foods. I believe they cause rapid growth of tumours. Maybe omega-3 supplements made from marine algae containing EPA could be an alternative to seafood for vegetarians.

Ceviche is a great way to serve seafood, a traditional dish from South and central America. The name describes seafood cured with lemon or lime juice. The acid in the juice changes the protein in the fish so it seems cooked, but no heat is applied.

The first time I made it for a party I got annoyed with squeezing eighty limes. It also took me a long time to fillet a red snapper. But my guests loved the ceviche.

I needed shortcuts. I did not want to use lemon juice

sold in bottles because it contains ascorbic acid that adds an unpleasant flavour. So I cured the fish overnight in synthetic vinegar, rinsed the cured fish and doused it in lemon vinaigrette. This worked perfectly. Instead of fresh fish, I now use frozen Basa fish fillets from Vietnam.

32 CEVICHE

I think everybody has to form his or her opinion about basa fish. Our oceans are overfished and polluted. You don't know how much fresh fish is contaminated.

Basa fish, also known as Panga and Pacific Dory, is one of the cheapest fishes available. Only small fishes like mackerels or anchovies cost less.

I only buy frozen fish fillets in packets that look well-closed. If you buy defrosted fish fillets, you have to use them immediately.

This is a great dish for parties because you can prepare big amounts with relative ease. However, you cannot keep this dish longer than one or two days in the fridge.

INGREDIENTS

(Serves 4)

- 1 kg frozen Basa fish fillets
- 1 litre synthetic vinegar
- Around 12 lemons or limes
- 100 ml extra virgin olive oil
- 3 or 4 fresh, big red chillies

- 1 bundle spring onions
- Salt
- Pepper

METHOD

Thaw fish fillets for two hours. They are easier to slice slightly frozen. Cut into slices around 1 centimetre thick, place into a container and cover with vinegar. The fish should be covered by vinegar so it cures evenly.

Close container and refrigerate overnight. Rinse thoroughly. Drain and arrange slices on a platter. Wash, clean and finely slice spring onions. Spread over fish. Wash chillies, chop finely and put into a glass with tight-fitting lid. Squeeze limes; add juice and a teaspoon salt to glass. Shake until salt has dissolved. Add olive oil and pepper and shake again to a fine emulsion. Spread vinaigrette over fish.

☞ **TIP:** You can take the taste of ceviche into different directions. You could make Mediterranean ceviche with oregano, thyme and garlic. Or you could add coriander and garam masala with ginger and/or cumin powder.

GIVE OMEGA-3 TO CHILDREN

Recently, the students in my son's school had to complete a questionnaire about their diet. My son was the only one in his class eating fish regularly. Few students liked seafood. One day, I invited his class home to make pizza together. Most of them made an icky face when they saw anchovies as pizza topping. Luckily, my son loves seafood and knows about its benefits. His favourite dish is seafood risotto.

Please try to get some omega-3 into your children. Our world needs intelligent people. Future generations will have to clean up the environment, develop energy sources that don't emit greenhouse gases and deal with artificial intelligence.

Few dishes combine healthy ingredients in such a fabulous way. This meal satisfies on many levels. It tastes great, delivers a hefty amount of omega-3 fatty acids, not to mention all the vitamins, minerals and phytonutrients from the vegetables. To keep it simple, I restrain my use of seafood to squids and prawns.

33 COLOURFUL SEAFOOD RISOTTO

A traditional seafood risotto can have any kind of fish. If you want to include mussels, clean them and fry them in a pan with a little bit of oil. Toss opened mussels into the risotto at the end of the cooking time; discard mussels that stay closed.

If you wish to incorporate fish, clean it and cut it into bite-size pieces. Add them to the risotto five minutes before the rice is cooked. You need Italian rice to cook a proper risotto. No other rice will give you the creamy texture of Arborio, Carnaroli or Vialone Nano rice.

INGREDIENTS

(Serves 4)

- 300 gms squids
- 300 gms prawns
- 1 cup rice
- 1 red bell pepper
- 1 yellow bell pepper
- 1 green bell pepper
- 2 stalks celery
- 1 bundle spring onions
- 1 carrot
- 1 medium beetroot
- 3 garlic cloves
- 1 packet tomato puree (200 ml)
- 4 tbsp olive oil
- Salt
- Pepper
- 3 cups water or fish stock

☞ **TIP:** If you want some zing in your risotto, add some fresh, chopped chillies when you start cooking.

METHOD

Skin and clean squids. Cut into bite-size pieces. Wash and devein prawns by cutting along their spine and pulling out dark strings.

Clean vegetables. Grate carrot and beetroot. Cube peppers and celery. Crush garlic. Italian rice for risotto needs eighteen minutes to be done. Keep this in mind when you want to incorporate different kinds of seafood.

Pour olive oil into a pot with heavy bottom that distributes heat evenly. Fry spring onions and celery. After two minutes, add squids, garlic and rice. Stir, then add one cup of liquid. Gradually add all liquid, tomato puree, carrot and beetroot. You don't want the cooking temperature drop too much by adding all liquid at once. You need a gentle simmering.

About five minutes before rice is done, incorporate bell peppers. At the end of the cooking time, add prawns. Season with salt and pepper.

Risotto should not turn into a stiff paste, but flow gently onto the plate. If necessary, add more liquid.

RISOTTO – A GIFT OF COLONIALISM

The veil of times gone by covers the history of riziculture in Italy, but some facts are known. The Romans knew rice but they cultivated it for medicinal purposes only. The Arabian invasion of parts of Europe established rice fields in Spain and Sicily. During the following centuries the popularity of rice grew among wealthy Italians.

In the 15th century, merchants cleared the Lombardy plains in northern Italy to grow rice. Venice, Milan and Ferrara made huge profits. The workers, many of them children, were kept practically as slaves. During the centuries, rice became a staple in this part of Italy. The cooking technique of risotto was invented some time along the way.

PROBLEMS OF SCIENTIFIC STUDIES

The problem with studying the effects of food on human bodies is the nature of our existence. Scientists cannot cut us up immediately after eating something to see the effect. They need to rely on long-term studies and these are only as reliable as the test subjects. Can you imagine sticking to a diet for the sake of a scientific study? I can, but only for one or two weeks at the most.

Over the years, we have listened to a lot of advice from experts that turned out to be wrong. We were not supposed to eat many eggs, coconuts and butter. I follow with interest what scientists discover but I trust myself. When something tastes delicious, it makes me happy for a little while – and that is healthy, no matter what.

You still find many sources that recommend being careful with eating prawns because of cholesterol. Studies have shown that eating prawns does not lead to dangerously high cholesterol levels. Long-term studies show there is no link between eating saturated fats and heart disease. But there are scientists who vehemently oppose these studies. They claim it is scientific truth that eating prawns leads to high cholesterol levels in the blood.

I think we should eat as many different foods as possible. Prawns deliver plenty of precious omega-3. My recipe for garlic prawns provides a sauce based on sherry. I like to serve them with organic brown rice.

34 GARLIC PRAWNS WITH BROWN RICE

In Goa you find organic red or brown rice from different producers. You need to cook it longer than white rice, but I think extra vitamins and minerals are worth it. You can make this recipe with any kind of prawns; I prefer medium-sized or big prawns. If you cannot find fresh prawns you can use two packets of frozen prawns.

INGREDIENTS

(Serves 4)

- 1 kg fresh prawns or 2 packets frozen prawns
- 3 tbsp cornstarch
- 1 bundle spring onions
- 6 big cloves garlic
- 5 tbsp olive oil
- 1 tbsp butter
- 100 ml sherry or dry white wine
- 100 ml water
- Salt
- Pepper
- 1½ cups brown rice

METHOD

Rinse and drain rice; place into a pressure cooker with three cups of water and one teaspoon salt. Boil for thirty minutes on low flame after first whistle.

Devein prawns and rinse well. Mix with cornstarch.

Clean and chop spring onions; crush garlic. Heat oil in a pan. Fry spring onions until translucent, then add garlic. Add wine and water. Bring to a boil, add prawns and simmer for 1 minute until sauce thickens. Add butter. Season with salt and pepper and serve immediately.

DON'T MISS OUT ON PRAWNS

The colour of prawns is called astaxanthin, a carotenoid with anti-inflammatory and antioxidant properties. It seems to lower colon cancer and immune-related problems of diabetes. No other seafood provides as much astaxanthin as prawns.

Selenium is essential for the functioning of enzymes. Lack of selenium increases the risk of heart failure and other cardiovascular diseases, type 2 diabetes and depression. Like other crustaceans, prawns contain a lot of protein, vitamin B12 and other B vitamins, and minerals such as copper, magnesium, phosphorus, and zinc.

BUTTER MYTH REMAINS

For decades, we were warned not to eat butter because of saturated fat. In the 1960s, the American Heart Association recommended cutting back on saturated fat because it furthers heart disease. For about half a century, this credo dominated the world, playing into the hands of margarine producers and manufacturers of high-cost, low-fat diet stuff.

A meta-analysis published in the *American Journal of Clinical Nutrition* in 2010 denied a link between saturated fat in the diet and coronary heart disease, stroke or cardiovascular disease. Plenty of experts now recommend butter, yet the myth remains. A few years ago, I had to listen to a harsh critique from a gym owner. When she heard how much butter goes into the making of the following tuna pâté, she called it unhealthy.

I believe that butter is healthy, especially uncooked butter as is used in this recipe – no matter what experts say. I base my opinion on the satisfaction my body derives from the taste of butter. I stumbled upon the recipe for tuna pâté during a family lunch in Milano, Italy. It melted in the mouth and left a satisfied feeling in the belly. Traditional cooking is as highly valued by my Italian family as their 300-year-old oak dinner table. When I asked my sister-in-law for the recipe, I was surprised by its simplicity.

35 TUNA PÂTÉ

This recipe is a winner. You need the best tuna you can find and an almost indecent amount of butter. You can also use smoked salmon for this dish.

INGREDIENTS

(Serves 12)

- 1 tin tuna in oil (about 250 gms fish)
- 250 gms butter
- Salt
- Pepper

METHOD

The only thing to remember is to use butter at room temperature. Open tin of tuna, drain and chop tuna finely in a blender. Gradually add butter and mix well. Season with salt and pepper. You can prepare this recipe with smoked salmon also. Just take equal amounts of fish and butter.

GOOD OLD BUTTER

Research shows that butter is healthy. There is good and bad cholesterol and butter is full of the good kind. Butter also provides plenty of vitamins, minerals and healthy fatty acids. If you manage to get your hands on butter from grass-fed cows, please go for it. This kind of butter is rich in omega-3. Butter also contains glycosphingolipids that protect the stomach from infections. Another plus of raw butter is the Wulzen factor: a hormone-like substance that protects stiffness in joints and makes sure that calcium reaches bones.

NO SHORTCUT TO NIRVANA

When you start eating omega-3 fatty acids regularly, don't expect immediate changes. Many experts recommend butter from grass-fed cows as an excellent source for omega-3 fatty acids. Eating the feel-good fat helps balance your mood but it is no shortcut to nirvana.

A significant difference in your emotional well-being takes time. Moments of calm content increase gradually. Eating fish regularly – together with serotonin snacks – definitely keeps the blues at bay. It does not guarantee a sunny mood

24/7 but I have experienced that I overcome low moments a lot easier. If you are concerned about heavy metals in fish, stick to small varieties like sardines and anchovies. Heavy metals accumulate in predators, not in small fish feeding on algae and phytoplankton. Treasure can be found at the bottom of the food chain.

CHAPTER 4

HAPPY BELLY, HAPPY MIND

Our bellies can make us happy or sad. A well-working belly contributes largely to a happy state of mind. People with digestive disorders tend to suffer from depression and anxiety also. By taking good care of our digestion we can influence the brain. Today, some doctors even cure depression by healing the digestive system. Naturally, the food that has to travel through your intestines largely influences its conditions.

Scientists underestimated the intelligence our bodies harbour for a long time. When we think of ourselves, we mostly consider our brain as the seat of our intelligence. But our so-called gut feeling delivers a kind of wisdom that has nothing to do with logic. When you listen to people talking about life-changing experiences, they often speak about their gut feeling, their instinct or their intuition.

Nowadays, many scientists call the digestive system the second brain. The precise name is Enteric Nervous System (ENS). Our intestines are around nine metres long and harbour many millions of neurons. They produce a wide range of hormones and around forty neurotransmitters, the same as found in the brain. The guts produce as much dopamine as the brain and the biggest part of serotonin in our bodies, about 95 per cent, is found there.

The ENS communicates with the brain extensively, in two ways. The brain can influence the guts and vice versa. This can be good or bad news. Constantly living under stress with high levels of cortisol damages the gut lining after some time. Studies have even shown that most children with stomach pains experience depression as adults. Luckily, by taking care of good digestion we can influence the brain.

I don't think that you can blame only a weak digestive system for depression. But I believe that you are more likely to enjoy a happy state of mind when your belly is working fine. If you suffer from bloating, weak digestion and stomach pains, you might want to get checked by a doctor for the following conditions: allergies, parasites, lack of stomach acid and enzymes, yeast infection, leaky gut syndrome and imbalances in the gut flora.

I believe people on a high fibre diet like plenty of whole grains, fruits and vegetables are happier and more alert.

In my kitchen I only use 'atta', the traditional Indian whole-wheat flour, rich in fibre. Another critical point is the gut flora. Did you know that we harbour ten times more bacteria (about 100 trillions) than our bodies have cells? Every human carries three to five pounds of bacteria in the belly. You can cultivate friendly bacteria in your intestines by eating yoghurt and other fermented products or lactobacillus supplements.

DIFFICULT RAPPORT WITH CURVES

I appreciate healthy motions every morning. During my first colonoscopy doctors told me that my guts are unusually long and winded. As a consequence, I am prone to constipation and flatulence. This also explains my round belly. My large digestive system needs space. The doctors recommended fibre-rich food and lactobacillus supplements. I have followed this advice for many years now and it has helped greatly.

For decades I struggled with my belly. As a teenager, I longed for a flat abdomen. Today, at around sixty kilograms, I can grab my belly fat between my fingers. Sometimes I wished this little roll would disappear. But with the years I have come to tolerate it. When I am in a good mood, I pat it gently.

Long gone are the days when I thought I need the perfect figure. At over fifty years, I don't have to compete with the looks of young women. Nobody likes ageing , but it also takes some pressure off. I have gained a lot of experience over the years making me more tolerant with others and myself. I could not have written this book at a younger age.

That does not mean I don't care about my figure or my looks, but we need to be forgiving and love ourselves. If we don't love our body, who else will?

Fibre-rich food keeps our bellies moving and in good shape. Fibres are found in whole grains, vegetables, fruits, nuts and legumes. All protein-rich foods like meat, seafood, dairy and eggs tend to be low in fibre. Only legumes provide plenty of proteins coupled with a lot of complex carbohydrates and fibre. I love legumes, especially the following recipe, a modern version of a traditional Greek recipe.

36 GIGANTES

These giant white beans are baked in a luscious tomato sauce. Some Greek housewives proclaim proudly that they add a full bottle of olive oil to one tray of gigantes. When you eat gigantes in Greece, the sauce resembles red tinted oil. This tastes delicious but only hardworking peasants need this kind of sustenance.

I have modified this dish to suit modern needs. I use considerably less olive oil and I hide as many vegetables as possible in my tomato sauce. Beetroot adds a lovely deep red tone to the sauce. Greeks bake the beans in the oven, which takes hours and kills most vitamins. I precook the beans, and bake them with the tomato sauce for around one hour.

Greeks eat gigantes as main course with a chunk of feta. Gigantes are also great for an antipasti buffet. I prepare a big tray, serve them as main dish and keep the leftovers in the fridge as a healthy snack.

INGREDIENTS

(Serves 8)

- 500 gm giant white beans
- 1 big tin of peeled Italian tomatoes (800 gm) or 1 kg fresh tomatoes
- 2 big carrots
- 2 medium beetroots
- 3 medium onions
- 8 big cloves garlic
- 2 bundles parsley

- 🌶 100 ml extra virgin olive oil
- 🌶 Vinegar
- 🌶 Salt
- 🌶 Pepper

METHOD

Soak gigantes in water overnight. Drain and rinse well. Place into a pressure cooker with water and cook for ten minutes on low flame after first whistle. It is easy to overcook gigantes, be careful.

Peel and chop vegetables. Drop fresh tomatoes into boiling water for 1 minute. Peel and chop them. Spread vegetables and olive oil over bottom of baking tray. Add drained gigantes and one cup of water and mix.

Bake for one hour at 200 degrees Celsius. Gigantes should soften without losing shape. Wash and chop parsley. Add shortly before beans are done. Add salt and pepper. Drizzle olive oil and chopped parsley over gigantes before serving.

A TRIBUTE TO LEGUMES

Legumes, or dried beans, are often underrated. All legumes are nutritional powerhouses, rich in folic acid, calcium, iron, potassium, zinc and antioxidants. They deliver a lot of proteins in combination with complex carbohydrates and fibre.

When you eat a meal of legumes, you ingest a source of energy that is getting released for many hours. Their high fibre content lowers blood cholesterol and encourages the growth of healthy bacteria in our intestines. Most legumes also contain protease inhibitors, substances that suppress the growth of cancer cells and tumours.

GUT-BRAIN CONNECTION

Did you ever realize you should have listened to bad feelings in your belly? Unfortunately, our second brain does not have a voice. It can only cause butterflies in the belly to warn us.

I still remember a beautiful day in March 1994 in Goa. The sun was shining and I wanted to drive from Anjuna to Ashvem Beach to meet some friends for lunch. In 1994, you had to take a ferryboat to reach this distant part of North Goa.

When I tried to start my bike, it resisted for a long time. After five minutes, I had to take a break. A vague feeling of unease had settled in my belly but I ignored it and finally drove off.

The day was wonderful and made me feel on top of the world. On the way back to Anjuna, a bus was coming towards me in a curve. I tried to steer my motorbike out of the way, lost control and landed in the bushes. My right leg scraped along the exhaust pipe, burning it severely. My wounds took over a month to heal. During my recovery I thought many times that I should have listened to my belly.

When I was young, nobody talked about instincts and gut feelings. We consider our brain as the seat of our intelligence. But our gut feeling is endowed with wisdom transcending logic. Life-changing experiences are often based on gut feeling or intuition.

A fibre-rich diet protects the digestive system and legumes provide plenty of fibre. The following recipe is an Indian version of the Greek national dish, fasolada. I make this soup with rajma beans, not white beans.

This soup looks different but it has the same comforting effect on the belly as the original. I always cook a big pot. You can store leftovers for several days in the fridge or freeze portions. Greeks usually serve it with feta. Turn it vegan by omitting the cheese.

37 INDIANIZED FASOLADA

This is a dish best served hot on a cool winter night. In the spirit of Indianizing I used dried Kashmiri chillies. This soup benefits greatly from a sprinkling with fresh coriander leaves.

INGREDIENTS

(Serves 8)

- 500 gm rajma beans
- 2 packets tomato puree (200 ml each) or 1 tin of peeled tomatoes
- 100 ml extra virgin olive oil
- 3 big carrots
- 2 stalks celery
- 1 beetroot
- 1 large red onion
- 3 garlic cloves
- 3 dried Kashmiri chillies

- 🍶 Vinegar
- 🍶 Salt
- 🍶 Pepper
- 🍶 Fresh coriander (optional)

METHOD

Soak beans overnight in water. Par boil beans 10 minutes in pressure cooker on low flame after first whistle to reduce cooking time.

Clean and chop vegetables finely. Crush garlic. Slice carrots because they should be visible in finished soup. Grate beetroot. I add beetroot to tomato sauces and soups because it intensifies red colour and adds sweetness.

Heat four tablespoons olive oil in a pot. Fry vegetables and chillies over medium heat until onions turn translucent. Add tomatoes and mix. Add drained beans and enough water to cover beans.

Gently simmer soup until beans are tender for thirty-five minutes. Add remaining olive oil and season with salt and pepper. Sprinkle with fresh coriander leaves and feta cheese.

RAJMA BEANS DETOXIFY THE BODY

Rajma and other dry beans are known as 'Phaseolus vulgaris', which means 'common beans'. They trace their origin to a common ancestor bean in Peru. Spanish explorers brought them to Europe in the 15th century and Portuguese traders introduced them to Asia.

Beans are an excellent source of protein and cholesterol-lowering fibre. A lot of this fibre is soluble, that means it dissolves in the stomach and slows down digestion. This prevents blood sugar levels from rising quickly after a meal, making beans a good choice for people with diabetes, insulin resistance or hypoglycaemia.

Rajma beans supply the trace mineral molybdenum that helps eliminate sulphites. Sulphites are preservatives found in many industrial foods. Large amounts of folate, magnesium, manganese, iron and niacin (vitamin B1) make legumes an excellent ingredient supporting a healthy heart, improving memory, boosting antioxidant defence and providing plenty of fat-free energy. If you want to lose weight, eat a lot of beans.

STOMACH PAIN

For decades, I suffered from stomach pains, annoying but not severe enough to see a doctor. A few cramps a day were part of my life. After my son had been diagnosed with food allergies, I did an allergy test too. It turned out that I am allergic to many food items, especially to dairy, yoghurt and cheese. Now I try to avoid these kinds of food, although I do love a good cheese.

Pain can have a rather benign reason like allergies or a severe reason like cancer. Pain in the body can be caused by pain in the soul, but that does not make it less worthy of an investigation.

During my teenage years my belly was almost constantly hurting. In Greece, I found a balance with food for the first time. I believe fibre-rich food played a major role. On the

Greek island Folegandros I discovered my first husband and also the wholesomeness of legumes.

When I was a teenager, the explosion of world population loomed like a dark cloud on the horizon. You still could visit museums and monuments without queuing for hours. Entry fees were affordable. You could find lonely beaches even without a yacht.

My life-changing beach on Folegandros is called Agios Nikolaos, named after the chapel towering over rocky cliffs. Pine trees, crippled by autumn storms, gave shadow. A group of students from Athens ran a bar there. They knew how to cook over campfire. On this beach I experienced Greek's simple cuisine for the first time.

38 CHICKPEA SOUP

The recipe for this chickpea soup, called revithia, could not be simpler. I always cook a big pot and freeze half of it.

INGREDIENTS

(Serves 8)

- 500 gm chickpeas
- 3 big onions
- 3 stalks fresh rosemary
- 6 tbsp extra virgin olive oil
- Salt
- Pepper
- Lime or lemon juice

METHOD

Soak chickpeas overnight. Rinse, place in a pot and cover with water. Bring water to a boil. Skim off froth forming on top. Boil chickpeas for fifteen minutes. Drain and rinse. This makes them easier to digest.

Clean and chop onions. Place into a pressure cooker with rosemary and drained chickpeas. Cover with water and boil for at least one hour.

You can also prepare this soup in a normal pot. Just boil chickpeas until soft.

To preserve nutrition of olive oil I add it towards the end of cooking time. Season with salt and pepper.

Serve soup with plenty of freshly squeezed lime juice and an extra drizzle of olive oil.

A TRIBUTE TO THE HUMBLE CHICKPEA

The chickpea – like all other members of the legumes family – offers a lot of proteins, minerals and fibre. Fibre helps to stabilize blood sugar levels, making chickpeas an excellent choice for diabetics and people with insulin resistance or hypoglycaemia. Chickpeas and their small cousin, Bengal gram, contain plenty of folic acid, manganese and iron which is needed for healthy bones and blood production. They deliver large amounts of the trace mineral molybdenum which flushes out the preservative sulphite from our bodies.

CALCULATING FIBRE? NO, THANKS

When I eat a lot of fibre, my digestion works well and I feel fine. Most food items contain soluble and insoluble fibre. Fruits, vegetables and nuts contain more insoluble fibres; whole grains and legumes more soluble. I think the recommendation of experts to eat twenty-five grams of fibre a day is useless. I believe in eating plenty of whole grains, legumes, fruits and vegetables, not calculating fibre amounts. I have better things to do with my time.

Recently, I found organic wheat berries. I decided to prepare them like a risotto with sun-dried tomatoes and mushrooms. For the first time I encountered wheat berries in Greece. When somebody dies, female relatives prepare a sweet called koliva with wheat berries. The boiled grains are mixed with nuts, pomegranate seeds, raisins and sugar piled. After the mass for the deceased, women distribute koliva.

39 WHEAT BERRIES RISOTTO STYLE

Wheat berries have a rich, earthen flavour. Sun-dried tomatoes and mushrooms echo this, but they need the contrast of green, fresh herbs and balsamic vinegar. You can serve this risotto as main dish with grated parmigiano or grana cheese or as side dish with chicken or fish.

INGREDIENTS

(Serves 4)

- 2 cups wheat berries
- 2 celery sticks

- 3 carrots
- 2 medium onions
- 3 cloves garlic
- 2 packets button mushrooms (400 gm)
- ½ cup sun-dried tomatoes
- 1 bundle fresh parsley or coriander
- 6 tbsp extra virgin olive oil
- 3 tbsp balsamic vinegar
- Salt
- Pepper

METHOD

Rinse wheat berries. Drain and place in a pressure cooker with four cups of water. Cook for forty minutes on low flame after first whistle.

Drain, but keep cooking liquid. Soak sun-dried tomatoes in hot water for fifteen minutes. Drain and keep water. Chop tomatoes, onions and celery. Crush garlic. Peel carrots and slice finely. Clean mushrooms.

Wash and chop fresh herbs. Place four tablespoons olive oil in a pot with heavy bottom. Fry onions until translucent; add drained wheat berries. Stir before adding celery and garlic.

Incorporate the drained water from the wheat berries and the sun-dried tomatoes. Simmer for fifteen minutes. Slice mushrooms. Stir mushrooms and carrots into risotto. Cook until wheat berries are tender. You might need to add a bit more water. Season with salt and pepper. Add herbs and balsamic vinegar. Drizzle with olive oil before serving.

RICH IN NUTRIENTS, LOW IN CALORIES

Wheat berries deliver the goodness of full grains, especially plenty of B and E vitamins. They also contain a lot of minerals, magnesium, phosphorus, selenium, manganese and copper combined with a lot of fibre.

FIBRE, THE BULK TO CHERISH

A gut-friendly diet delivers loads of fibre, material for a healthy gut lining with friendly bacteria. Both, soluble and insoluble fibre, help the digestive process. Soluble fibre produces a gel that slows down the digestive process, makes you feel full and balances blood sugar levels. In the large intestines, bacteria can digest this fibre. This causes an acidic milieu that kills germs. Insoluble fibre stimulates the movements of the muscles around the intestines.

You need to drink a lot with fibre-rich food to help the process.

When I am constipated, I cook the following bean burgers. Burgers provide easy, fast dinners and you can make them from anything you fancy. I don't like to stuff them into a soft, chewy bun. I dish them up with a salad or vegetables. My men, the meat lovers, prefer burgers made from beef or chicken.

40 MINI BURGERS

I use split Bengal gram, split baby chickpeas, for this recipe. Bengal gram is easy to digest and does not need soaking overnight. For these burgers you need the right consistency.

Mini burgers cook fast and look pretty. I have used traditional Indian flavours in the recipe.

INGREDIENTS

(Makes 20 mini or 8 big burgers)

- 2 cups split Bengal gram
- ½ cup besan flour
- 1 cup oats
- 1 big or 2 small eggs
- 1 bundle spring onions
- 1 big carrot
- 3 cloves garlic
- ½ cup fresh coriander
- 6 tbsp oil
- 1 tbsp salt
- 1 tbsp garam masala
- 1 tbsp ground red chillies
- 1 tbsp ground cumin
- 1 tbsp ground coriander seeds
- Burger buns

METHOD

Soak Bengal gram for one hour in water. Drain and rinse. Place into a pressure cooker with water and cook on low flame for thirty minutes after first whistle. Drain.

Clean spring onions, carrots, garlic and coriander. Put into a blender and chop finely. Add Bengal gram, besan flour, oats, egg and spices, and blend. Scrape down the sides of blender to achieve an even result.

Season with salt and pepper. Spread oil over a cookie sheet. Form small patties. An ice cream scoop works well for this. Bake for forty minutes at 190 degrees Celsius. Turn after twenty minutes to brown both sides.

BENGAL GRAM – THE RIGHT CHOICE ON SO MANY LEVELS

Large amounts of folate, magnesium, manganese, iron and niacin (vitamin B1) make Bengal gram an excellent ingredient supporting a healthy heart, improving memory, boosting antioxidant defence and providing plenty of fat-free energy. If you want to lose weight, eat a lot of beans.

OUR BIOCHEMICAL SERVICE STATION

Hundreds of different kinds of bacteria live happily in the large intestine, providing biochemical services that our body cells are not able to perform. But they need to be fed. Most carbohydrates, proteins and fats get absorbed into the blood stream before they reach the large intestine.

Fibre reaches the large intestine and provides nourishment for the bacteria. In turn, these bacteria produce nutrients for the body – short-chain fatty acids like butyrate that support the cells in the colon. They are vital for a strong immune system and reduce inflammation in the intestines.

Resistant starches have recently become fashionable, especially in the USA. They reach the large intestine intact. Grains, seeds, legumes, green bananas, raw potatoes, cooked and cooled rice and potatoes contain these kinds of starches. I think when you eat a fibre-rich diet you provide enough resistant starches for your bacteria. If you suffer from severe digestive disorders like ulcers, Crohn's Disease or leaky gut syndrome you might want to investigate resistant starches.

Legumes deliver resistant starches, especially chickpeas. Falafel, the chickpea fritter from the Middle East, was named several times when I asked my friends for their favourite dishes.

41 FALAFEL

With horror I remember the first time I tried to make falafel. They completely fell apart, an ugly, oily mess. This dish dates back to ancient times. Copts in Egypt made legumes. These early Christians believed that human beings should live as vegetarians.

INGREDIENTS

(Makes 30)

- 2 cups dry chickpeas
- 2 eggs
- 4 tbsp whole wheat flour
- 1 onion
- 5 cloves garlic
- 1 bundle parsley or coriander (or both)
- 2 tbsp ground cumin

- 1 tbsp ground coriander
- Ground chillies
- Pepper
- Salt
- Oil for deep-frying

FOR TAHINI

- ½ cup tahini
- ¼ cup (50 ml) lemon or lime juice
- 2 small cloves garlic
- 2 tbsp extra virgin olive oil
- Salt
- Water

METHOD

Soak chickpeas overnight. Rinse and place in a blender. Chop onion, crush garlic. Wash parsley and/or coriander and chop.

Add onions, garlic, herbs and spices to chickpeas and grind. Scrape down the sides to achieve a smooth paste.

Add eggs and flour and blend. Fork through mix and remove any pieces of chickpeas. Refrigerate for two hours.

Heat oil in a wok or deep fryer. Form mix into small balls. Check temperature with one test falafel. It should take two to three minutes to brown on one side. Fry falafel in batches of five or six. Drain on kitchen towels. Serve immediately.

For tahini sauce, crush garlic. Place tahini into a bowl and incorporate lemon juice, olive oil and garlic. Add one or two tablespoons water while stirring to get a thick cream. Season with salt and pepper.

CHRISTIAN FRITTER BECOMES NATIONAL SNACK-FOOD IN ISRAEL

Yemenite immigrants in Israel were the first to stuff falafel together with sauces and vegetables into pita bread. Today, falafel has turned into the unofficial national snack food of Israel. I ate them for the first time twenty years ago in Goa.

Two decades later, I managed to prepare decent falafel. Always dish up falafel with a dipping sauce. In Israel, falafels are served with hummus and tahini sauce.

PHYTIC ACID, FRIEND OR FOE?

Recently, the paleo diet has attracted many followers. It warns us not to eat whole grains, nuts and legumes. The reason is phytic acid. It preserves the seeds of a plant until conditions are ripe for sprouting.

Believers in the paleo diet don't eat grains at all because of phytic acid. Some scientists agree that phytic acid can block the uptake of minerals. Some nutritionists recommend fermenting or soaking all seeds.

Honestly, I never got around to try this because it seems so tedious. I have eaten whole grains and legumes all my life and never noticed a lack of something.

Many experts disagree with the propagators of the paleo diet. They think that phytic acid applies its antioxidation properties in our guts. Some even say it might fight cancer.

My belly tells me that nuts are yummy; I like them without soaking.

My tummy also appreciates any kind of legumes, but they need to be cooked well. The following salad delivers everything I want in a recipe. It is easy to prepare and loaded with nutrition. You can serve it as main dish or starter, put it on a buffet or just keep it in the fridge as a snack.

42 SPICY RED BEANS SALAD

I discovered this salad long ago at the brunch buffet of my best friend's hotel. She owns a 400-year-old mansion close to Regensburg, nestled at the banks of the small river Vils, surrounded by limestone rocks. Every Sunday she serves brunch.

INGREDIENTS

(Serves 4)

- 200 gm red rajma beans
- 2 big, green peppers
- 2 big, red onions
- 1 cup boiled corn kernels
- 6 fresh, red Thai chillies
- 3 tbsp red wine vinegar
- 5 tbsp olive oil
- Vinegar
- Salt
- Pepper

METHOD

Soak beans overnight. Drain and rinse. Cook for thirty minutes in a pressure cooker after the first whistle and up to two hours in a normal pot. Drain. Wash green peppers and slice finely. Peel and chop onions in a blender.

Wash and chop chillies. Combine beans with vegetables in a bowl. Dissolve half a teaspoon salt in red wine vinegar and blend with olive oil. Add black pepper.

Pour dressing over salad and mix well. Marinate for one hour before serving.

ONIONS

Onions come in many colours and flavours, from very strong to mildly sweet. They belong to the lily family, the same family as garlic, leeks, chives, scallions and shallots. They contain a lot of thiosulphinates, sulphides, sulphoxides and other odouriferous sulphur compounds, which cause your eyes to tear up when cutting them.

Thiosulphinates kill many bacteria, including bacillus subtilis, salmonella, and coli bacteria. Onions prevent cardiovascular diseases because they diminish the risk of blood clots and protect against stomach and other cancers. They improve lung function, especially in asthmatics.

Like garlic, onions need oxygen to develop certain beneficial compounds. After chopping, let them rest for at least ten minutes before cooking them.

HIDDEN HYPOCRISY EVERYWHERE

Growing up, feminism was not an issue. I did not feel treated differently from my brothers. All over the world, women don't enjoy equal rights. My mother taught only me how to iron men's shirts, not my brothers. My father told me every man wants to marry a virgin. This attitude made me recoil in anger. Why is sex spoiling a woman, making her damaged goods? Luckily, I never met a man who wanted a virgin. Only gradually I discovered a lot of globally accepted hypocrisy towards women.

Holding women to different standards than men is so embedded in our brain that we tend to overlook it. Male dominance played a major part with my eating disorders. I rebelled in the only way I could, a self-destructive one. Because I starved during teenage years, I have low bone density. If your children refuse food, please take it seriously.

I could not imagine living with a man who insists that I cook daily. I want my son to see women as human beings with equal rights.

43 FIERCE LENTIL SALAD

My favourite Indian lentil is whole masoor dal. I like its earthy flavour and the bright orange core, the perfect base for an unusual salad. French cuisine features lentil salad made with lentils from Puy-en-Velay, a city in Central France. The French, gifted in self-advertisement, have declared these lentils the best in the world, the 'Beluga' of legumes.

Good vinegar and smoked aromas underline the aroma of lentils. For the smokiness I added bacon and its rendered drippings. For a vegetarian version I substitute the bacon with smoked cheese and extra olive oil.

For fierceness, I add red Thai chillies. Be careful not to overcook the lentils. You don't want it mushy.

INGREDIENTS

(Serves 4)

- 1½ cups brown whole masoor dal
- 100 gm bacon and/or smoked cheese
- 2 celery sticks
- 1 leek
- 1 bundle spring onions
- 2 green bell peppers
- 10 red Thai chillies
- 4 garlic cloves
- 3 tbsp extra virgin olive oil (or 7 tbsp for vegetarian version)
- 3 tbsp red wine vinegar
- 2 tbsp balsamic vinegar
- Salt
- Pepper

METHOD

Soak lentils for one hour, rinse, cover with water and cook until just soft, around thirty to forty minutes. I use a normal pot to control cooking.

Clean and cut spring onions and leeks, crush garlic. Clean and cube green bell peppers and celery sticks. Heat olive oil in a pan; fry onions and leeks until translucent. Add celery cubes and garlic and fry for three minutes. Slice chillies and bacon. Fry bacon until crunchy and all fat has rendered. Keep bacon on a plate lined with kitchen towels. Deglaze bacon fat with vinegar.

Place lentils into a bowl; add vegetables, chillies and deglazed fat, and mix. Season with salt and pepper. Top salad with the bacon bits and serve.

For vegetarian version, dice cheese and make vinaigrette with crushed garlic.

LENTILS, SMALL POWERHOUSES

This small legume offers a wealth of nutrition with a long history. Archaeologists have found 8000 years old lentil seeds in the Middle East. Lentils are even mentioned in the Bible. They don't need to be soaked overnight, and they easily absorb flavours from spices. They contain a lot of fibre and minerals, complex carbohydrates and plenty of protein without any fat.

Lentils provide two B vitamins and big amounts of six important minerals, among them folate, magnesium and iron. Folate is especially important for pregnant women as it helps forming the nervous system of the unborn baby. Magnesium relaxes the walls of arteries and veins, thus improving the flow of blood, oxygen and nutrients throughout the body. The iron in lentils helps the body to form blood as it is a part of haemoglobin, the red blood cells which transport oxygen through the body.

TRAVEL-INSPIRED TASTE BUDS

My German upbringing shaped my psyche but not my taste buds. When I was a child, we spent holidays at the seaside every summer, either in France or Italy. I discovered early on that I loved different cuisines. We often returned home and tried our hand at different dishes. For example, my mother learnt how to make a pretty good thin crust pizza. Mediterranean cuisine remains my favourite although I like dishes from all over the world.

Travelling has always inspired my cooking. I first came across hummus in 1986 in Cyprus, an island in the Mediterranean, while wandering through crooked lanes in the centre of the capital Nicosia bordered by old houses. We stopped for lunch at a tiny restaurant run by a Lebanese with a big belly and a huge moustache. The kebab arrived with hummus and I fell in love with it.

44 HUMMUS

Modern media had an enormous impact on our culture. They have opened our taste buds to new experiences. Indians enjoy an ever-growing variety of cuisines. Hummus is one dish that has conquered the world. It always disappears quickly when I serve it at a party. I always prepare a big amount and then freeze portions.

INGREDIENTS

(Serves 8)

- 1 cup chickpeas
- 2 tbsp tahini
- 4 tbsp lemon or lime juice
- 3 tbsp olive oil
- 2 cloves garlic
- Salt
- Pepper
- ½ cup cooking liquid

METHOD

Soak chickpeas overnight. Drain, rinse and boil in a pressure cooker. Cook it for forty-five minutes on low flame after the first whistle.

Drain chickpeas, but save half a cup of cooking liquid. Place chickpeas with lemon juice, tahini, crushed garlic and olive oil into a blender. Season with salt and pepper; add some cooking liquid and blend to a smooth paste. It will thicken in fridge.

☞ **WARNING:** Chickpeas can cause severe allergic reactions.

HUMMUS WITH THE MAGIC OF SESAME

Hummus not only delivers plenty of fibre, vitamins and minerals, it also provides the wealth of sesame in tahini, a paste made from ground sesame seeds. In early Hindu legend, the tiny sesame seeds symbolize immortality and it is regarded as the supreme ingredient. The seeds contain two unique substances, sesamin and sesamolin, which avert high blood pressure and protect the liver. They are full of precious minerals like manganese and copper, and they are a good source of calcium, magnesium, iron, phosphorus, vitamin B1, zinc and dietary fibre. The high amount of phytosterols in sesame is another vital feature. Sufficient intake of phytosterols reduces cholesterol levels, thus strengthening the immune system and decreasing the risk of certain cancers.

SEROTONIN SNACKS BOOST MOOD

For baking my mother used only white flour. During the 1970s in Germany, magazines started to write about benefits of whole grains. A few years later, I found whole-wheat pasta for the first time in a supermarket. I was always keen on experimenting with food and its effect on our body.

'Food is like a pharmaceutical compound that affects the brain,' wrote Fernando Gómez-Pinilla, a professor of neurosurgery and physiological science at the University of California (UCLA). This sentence applies to high-fibre bread rolls, the following recipe. If used correctly, bread rolls and other foods high in carbohydrates, and low in fat and protein can improve serotonin levels in the brain. Eaten at night, they improve sleep.

About 90 per cent of all the serotonin in our bodies is found in and around our digestive system. In our brain, serotonin delivers calm, confident feelings and regulates appetite.

It is difficult to raise serotonin levels in the brain. Serotonin supplements don't reach the brain because its molecules are too big to pass the blood-brain barrier. Only tryptophan and and its metabolite 5-hydroxytryptophan, its building blocks, can cross this barrier – under certain conditions. This barrier is a membrane with chemical 'doors'. Several amino acids compete with tryptophan to enter through this door.

INSULIN

Avoid high spikes in insulin levels; use them in a controlled way to raise serotonin levels. Some hours after a protein-rich meal, a carbohydrate snack releases a small spike of insulin. This snack should contain as little fat and protein as possible. It can have sugar – you could eat whole-wheat rolls topped with jam or honey – but not butter. Two slices of toast deliver the perfect dose. Fat-free crackers, bread sticks, pita bread, rice cakes or crackers, and even marshmallows work as serotonin snack. You need at least thirty grams of carbohydrates for the desired effect. Carbohydrates from fruit do not deliver.

The carbohydrates release the hormone insulin from the pancreas. Insulin pushes proteins from blood vessels into organs – except tryptophan. At this point it can enter the brain and be converted there into serotonin. Don't eat anything for half an hour after a serotonin snack. Don't expect any immediate results. It takes at least two weeks to build up serotonin levels.

In their book *The Serotonin Power Diet,* Judith J. Wurtman and Nina T. Frusztajer recommend three snacks a day to raise serotonin levels, the first snack: one hour before lunch, the second: three to four hours after lunch, and the third: two to three hours after dinner. After two weeks cut down to two snacks a day, an hour before and three to four hours after lunch. After nine weeks eat only one snack three to four hours after lunch. At meal times eat tryptophan-rich foods combined with a lot of vegetables and fruits.

CARBOHYDRATES

I have tried serotonin snacks without following the diet prescribed in the book and it worked for me. After sticking to serotonin snacks for some weeks, I slept a lot better. Melatonin, the hormone that regulates our sleep, is made from serotonin. When you raise serotonin levels, you also improve melatonin levels.

Even now, I eat a carbohydrate snack two to three hours after dinner to help me sleep better. I also sneak in serotonin snacks at the proper time during the day. To raise serotonin levels, you also need B vitamins and omega-3 fatty acids. B vitamins help to synthesise serotonin in the brain. Whole grains, nuts, seeds, fruits, vegetables, fish and meat provide plenty of B vitamins. Sugar needs B vitamin, magnesium and calcium to be digested without delivering any nutrients. That's why it is called an empty carbohydrate.

45 BREAD ROLLS

I have experimented for years making bread without success. Then I watched a TV show about French bakers crafting baguette. Nowhere in the world does bread smell as lovely as in France. I learned two things: it takes two days to make baguette, and you sprinkle bread with water during baking. Voilà! For the first time, I really liked my rolls.

INGREDIENTS

(Makes 24)

- 1 kg whole wheat flour (atta)
- 200 gm oats or wheat bran
- 2 packets dry yeast
- 2 tbsp sugar
- 1 tbsp salt
- Water
- Sesame or poppy seeds (optional)

☞ **TIP:** The rolls keep well in the fridge for up to three days. I freeze rolls that I don't need immediately.

METHOD

Yeast is a fungus, which loves warm moisture. Take half a cup of water; add two tablespoons of sugar and yeast. Wait until bubbles start to form.

Place flour and bran into a bowl. Dig a hole in the middle and pour yeast mixture into it. Cover with flour and wait until yeast bubbles over. Sprinkle with salt, place a container with water close by and dive in with your hands.

You need to knead yeast with flour and water, at least 750 millilitres, until you have a smooth dough. The longer you work it, the better. It needs at least five minutes of kneading. I smash it 200 times onto my granite kitchen counter. Cover dough with wet cloth and let it rise for about two hours until it has doubled in size.

Cover a cookie sheet with a silicone sheet or baking paper and make twenty-four little rolls. Sprinkle with sesame or poppy seeds and press them into dough. Cover rolls with wet cloth. Let rise for at least two hours again.

I bake rolls for one and a half hours at lowest temperature (180 degrees Celsius). After three quarters of an hour, spread wet cloth over rolls. Repeat at least two more times. Flip rolls ten minutes before end of baking.

I BELIEVE IN WHOLE WHEAT

Wheat, an ancient grain, played a role in many rituals. It plays an important part in feeding my family. In my kitchen I only use whole wheat flour. White flour lacks the bran and the germ of the wheat grain, the parts holding B vitamins and minerals.

Studies show that eating whole grains helps avoid type 2 diabetes and gallstones. I have not noticed any negative consequences from using whole wheat flour – never mind phytic acid.

WEIGHT LOSS WITHOUT DIET

Losing weight is never easy. When I suffered from anorexia, I ate miniscule portions. When I want to lose weight today – usually after holidays – I avoid sugar, alcohol and white flour, and try to eat small portions. The thing to remember is to keep blood sugar levels balanced and insulin levels low.

Sugary sweets and other empty carbohydrates may taste wonderful, but should remain an indulgence. When you eat sugar and white flour, rice and starch play yoyo with your blood sugar and insulin levels. Sugar and empty carbohydrates make blood sugar levels rise quickly, causing the pancreas to release insulin. Our cells cannot absorb glucose without this hormone. Thanks to insulin, the cells use the glucose floating around in the blood stream and blood sugar levels fall quickly. At this point, you feel the urge to eat more sugar and the cycle starts again.

Unfortunately, insulin tells the body to store extra calories in fat. Even worse, high insulin levels suppress two other important hormones: glucagons and growth hormones, responsible for burning fat and muscle growth. High insulin levels not only make us fat, they hinder the body to lose fat.

If you eat a lot of sugar every day, you take a shortcut to many diseases. Many studies link sugar with mood disorders like depression and panic attacks. Over time your body becomes less sensitive to insulin. Constant high levels of blood sugar cause type 2 diabetes, renal malfunction, foot ulcers and other diseases.

For losing weight, the following recipe is my secret weapon. When I have put on weight during holidays, I stick to crackers.

46 CRACKERS WITH SALSA DIP

These crackers not only taste great, thanks to the flax and sesame seeds, they are nutritious and keep your digestion going. If you want a healthy snack, serve them with spicy salsa dip. For lunch, I love them with any kind of pâté. You can keep them for up to two weeks.

INGREDIENTS

(Makes 16)

- 5 cups whole-wheat flour
- 1 cup oat bran
- 5 tbsp olive oil or cold pressed coconut oil
- 1 cup curd
- 100 gm flaxseeds
- 100 gm sesame seeds
- 1 tbsp salt
- Water

SPICY SALSA DIP

(Serves 4)

- 4 big, red tomatoes
- 1 red or yellow bell pepper
- 4 fresh, green chillies
- 1 tsp balsamic vinegar
- 1 tbsp olive oil
- ½ tsp sugar
- Salt
- Freshly grated pepper
- Any kind of herb you like

METHOD

Grind flaxseeds in a blender. Put dry ingredients in a bowl and mix well. Add oil, curd and enough cold water to make smooth dough. Knead dough for five minutes and let rest for ten minutes before rolling out.

Dust a flat surface with flour. Roll out a piece of dough as thinly as possible in the required shape. Place on a cookie sheet and score lines with a sharp knife. These lines help to break crackers after baking.

The amount given is enough to cover four cookie sheets. Bake crackers for twenty minutes at 200 degrees Celsius. They should be hard, dry and slightly browned. Let them cool down, then break into pieces.

Immerse tomatoes for 1 minute in boiling water. Remove skin, seeds and any white pieces from stalk. Cut flesh into cubes and put into a bowl. Clean and cube bell peppers. Slice chillies. Wash herbs, chop finely and add vegetables to the bowl. Add sugar, vinegar, oil and salt and pepper. Mix well.

TINY SIZE, MIGHTY CONTENT

Flaxseeds contain a huge amount of nutritious substances. 100 grams of flaxseeds provide twenty-eight grams of fibre! 100 grams of whole wheat flour deliver only ten grams. Nothing keeps your digestive system going like flaxseeds. Always drink enough when you eat something prepared with flaxseeds. The fibres need liquid to expand and push their way through the intestines, cleaning them at the same time. The high amount of fibre stabilises blood sugar levels and prevents colon cancer. Flaxseeds also have a beneficial effect on persons with high blood pressure, asthma and diabetes. Experts call these tiny seeds 'superfood' due to the large amounts of B vitamins, folate, calcium, iron, potassium, selenium and zinc they contain.

PREBIOTICS AND PROBIOTICS

Another important part of a belly friendly diet is yoghurt or drinks with probiotic bacteria. Prebiotics, on the other hand, are the fibres that nourish the friendly bacteria in the gut, the probiotics.

I am allergic to yoghurt so I get my gut-friendly bacteria from lactobacillus capsules. Whenever I experience bloating, I take lactobacillus.

When you combine sugar with plenty of fibre, like in these bran muffins, you don't play yoyo with blood sugar levels. When the blood sugar levels drop, the energy from the complex carbohydrates arrives and you don't feel like eating another sweet quickly. That's why I use only whole wheat flour for baking sweets rather than white flour.

47 BRAN MUFFINS

These oat and bran muffins may not be the peaks of culinary accomplishment, but they take care of your intestines like few other foods. It has taken many experiments in my kitchen to develop a recipe that does not resemble cardboard. Cold-pressed coconut oil makes these muffins moist.

INGREDIENTS

(Makes 12)

- 2½ cups oat bran
- 1½ cups whole wheat flour
- ½ cup coconut oil
- 2 eggs
- 1½ cups milk
- 1 cup dried raisins
- 1 cup sugar
- 1 tbsp vanilla essence
- 1 tbsp cinnamon
- 1 tsp ground clove
- 1 tbsp baking powder

METHOD

Grease muffin moulds and line with paper or use silicone muffin moulds. Preheat oven to 190 degrees Celsius.

Clean and rinse raisins. Break eggs into a bowl and add sugar, cinnamon, cloves, vanilla essence and/or cardamom. Stir well.

Add milk and oil. Stir again.

Add oat bran and mix. Let it sit for ten minutes. If dough turns very thick, add more liquid.

Mix flour with baking powder and stir into dough. Fill muffin moulds and bake at 190 degrees for twenty to twenty-five minutes. A toothpick inserted in the middle should come out clean.

FIBRE SOURCES

Oats and oat bran are a great source of fibre because they have soluble and insoluble fibre in equal amounts: 100 grams of oats contain eleven grams of fibre. The soluble fibre of oats called beta-glucan is especially effective in binding cholesterol. Experts recommend eating at least eighteen grams of fibre a day. Fibre content of different foods (per 100 gm) is listed below.

- Whole grain spaghetti: 8.4 gm
- Whole grain bread: 6.3 gm
- Peas: 3.4 gm
- Apples: 1.8 gm
- Brown rice: 1.8 gm
- Oranges: 1.7 gm of fibre per 100 gm
- Mushrooms: 1.5 gm of fibre per 100 gm
- Onions: 1.4 gm of fibre per 100 gm

EMBRACE SUGAR AND SWEETS

Avoiding sugar completely would be best but I think this is too much to ask of anybody. Most people, myself included, suffer under harsh restrictions. I have grown up with 'Kaffee und Kuchen' (coffee and cake) in the afternoon, a dietary nightmare. Most cultures embrace sugar. My mother baked two to three cakes every weekend. A sugar-rich dessert followed every festive lunch. To indulge in our not-so-healthy dietary fancies can make us happy too. I do believe we should not eat much sugar. Sugar makes fat, especially commercial substances like high fructose corn syrup.

I always try to impart many healthy ingredients in my sweets like oats in the following recipe.

48 CHOCOLATE-CHIP COOKIES

These chocolate-chip cookies always disappear quickly. They contain sugar and lots of dark chocolate, but also rolled oats, whole wheat flour and walnuts. They are free of chemical additives found in commercial cookies – a big plus in my book.

INGREDIENTS

(Makes 24)

- 5 eggs
- 2 cups icing sugar
- 1 cup whole wheat flour
- 5 cups rolled oats
- 100 gm walnuts
- 250 gm dark cooking chocolate or chocolate chips
- 150 gm butter
- 1 tbsp vanilla essence
- Butter to grease 2 cookie sheets

☞ TIP: I have a gas oven with heat only from the bottom. To bake sweets evenly, I end the baking time with two to five minutes of grilling.

METHOD

The easiest way to obtain chocolate chips in India is making them. Place chocolate on a chopping board; shave off chocolate chips with a big knife. Chop walnuts roughly.

Melt butter. Crack eggs into a bowl. Add sugar and vanilla essence and whip with a hand mixer.

Incorporate flour and two cups of rolled oats. Add melted butter and stir well. Adjoin remaining oats, chocolate chips and walnuts. The dough should be rather firm.

Grease two cookie sheets with butter. Place heaps of dough on sheets. Leave enough space between cookies: they spread out quite a bit. Bake for twenty minutes on lowest flame.

SURPRISE? COCOA IS HEALTHY

Theobroma Cacao, the official scientific name of the tree, promises delight. Theobroma, an ancient Greek word, literally means 'food of the gods'. The word cacao probably was formed by the Olmec Indians around 1000 BC. The Aztecs ground cocoa beans and turned them into 'xocoatl'. We all know that chocolate makes us happy but this is not the only advantage that its key ingredient cocoa delivers. Studies show that it contains more than three times the flavonoids found in green tea. Chocolate is also a good source of copper and magnesium, which helps to regulate heartbeat and blood pressure.

The flavonoids of cocoa help to decrease blood pressure; they improve circulation and have a positive effect on blood vessels, preventing cardiovascular diseases. Furthermore, cocoa improves digestion and stimulates the kidneys.

THE MAGIC WINDOW

You can eat sweets without causing a peak in blood sugar and insulin levels after a workout. High profile bodybuilding experts like Jim Stoppani, PhD, and Mike Roussell, PhD recommend eating simple carbohydrates after exercise. Some experts call this the 'Magic Window'. Muscles absorb sugar immediately after a serious workout. You should raise your normal heart rate by at least 60 per cent for around thirty minutes. Checking your heart rate per minute is easy. Take your pulse and count it for ten seconds with the help of a stopwatch. Most mobile phones have stopwatches. Multiply the result with six. Add 60 percent and you know the heart rate for earning sweets. Cardio machines in gyms tell you the heart rate or you can use a heart rate monitor.

If you breathe so heavily that you cannot talk, you are in the zone. You can ease up once you have worked up a sweat. But keep your heart pounding. The magic window lasts for half an hour after the workout.

One of my favourite sweet indulgences remains apple pie. My recipe is strongly influenced by a Dutch friend. She was living with her husband in Utrecht, in a house with laced curtains, small rooms and blue-white porcelain. She made an apple pie that kept you warm during a cold storm.

49 APPLE PIE

For a long time I struggled with short crust for pies. Thanks to research I have figured out the technique. Use butter ice-cold, touch the flour as gently as possible and stop working when crumbs form. Pack the dough into cling film and let it rest for half an hour. The decisive step is rolling out between cling film. In this way you can achieve a thin layer of crunchy and flaky crust.

INGREDIENTS

(For a 30 cm/12 in pie form)

- 250 gm butter
- 5½ cups flour
- Ice-cold water
- 3 cups sugar
- 1.5 kg apples
- 100 gm raisins
- 100 gm almonds
- ½ tbsp ground cloves
- 3 tbsp ground cinnamon
- 1 tbsp vanilla essence
- Salt
- 1 egg yolk
- Butter to grease the pie form

METHOD

Cut butter into cubes. Place flour into a bowl; add one cup

sugar, one tablespoon vanilla essence, a pinch of salt and one tablespoon cinnamon. Blend with a spoon. Keep cold water handy. Add butter cubes from the fridge. Rub flour and butter together. Add cold water gradually. Stop when mixture resembles crumbs sticking together. Movement activates gluten in flour that turns short crust hard. Wrap dough in cling film and let it rest for half an hour.

Quarter and peel apples, cut out core and slice. Clean and rinse raisins. Put apples, raisins, two tablespoons cinnamon, ground cloves and remaining sugar into a bowl and mix. Grease pie form.

Place a bit more than half of dough between two sheets of cling film. Roll it out with a rolling pin to a size big enough to cover bottom and sides of pie dish. Gently push it into pie form. Grind almonds and spread over bottom of pie. Add apples. Press overlapping pieces of dough over apples. Roll remaining dough to size of pie form and cover apples. Press down and cut around pie form. Brush beaten egg yolk over pie. Bake for seventy-five minutes at lowest temperature.

APPLES TACKLE HEAVY METALS

Apples offer so many nutrients that this fruit should not be missing from any diet. But there is a drawback. In India, it is impossible to find organically grown apples. Pesticide residues poison skin of conventionally grown apples.

A peeled medium apple provides around three grams of soluble and insoluble fibre. Apple's insoluble fibre hooks up with bad cholesterol in the digestive tract, pushing it out from the body. Apple's soluble fibre, pectin, hangs on to heavy metals and shows them the way out. Both fibres stimulate bowel movement and ease constipation. Apples contain a lot of antioxidants and vitamin C also.

IRRELEVANT GLYCEMIC INDEX

The glycemic index is another hip thing in health conscious circles. It shows how quickly your body absorbs carbohydrates. Sugar has the highest glycemic index. I compare the glycemic index to calorie content – irrelevant information in daily life. I prefer to listen to my body.

The glycemic index can be misleading, only important for diabetics who inject insulin. The glycemic index of potatoes and brown rice is as high as that of white flour or rice; they deliver much more nutrition. Carrots have a high glycemic index too although they are rich in vitamins, minerals, carotenoids and fibre. When you combine sugar with complex carbohydrates like nuts you improve the glycemic index from sweets. But in the end, who cares?

50 CARROT CAKE

The first time my mother baked a carrot cake – about forty years ago or so – it was considered an exotic sweet in Germany. Actually, it is a resurrected one. Carrots have been used in cakes since the Middle Ages, when sweeteners were scarce and expensive. British housewives rediscovered carrot cake during the Second World War when sugar was missing. In the 1960s this cake found its way to the USA and has become a standard worldwide. I like carrot cake light and moist with a dusting of icing sugar.

INGREDIENTS

(For a 27 cm round baking dish)

- 4 eggs
- 2 cups sugar
- 4 medium carrots
- 2 cups flour
- 200 gm almonds
- ½ cup coconut oil
- 1 tbsp vanilla essence
- 2 tbsp cinnamon powder
- 1½ tbsp baking powder
- Butter to grease the baking dish
- 1½ cups icing sugar

METHOD

Grease the baking dish with butter. Preheat oven to 190 degrees Celsius.

Peel and grate carrots in a blender. Grind almonds. Crack eggs in a mixing bowl. Add vanilla essence, cinnamon and sugar, and stir with an electric hand mixer to a pale cream. Add carrots, coconut oil and ground almonds, and combine.

Mix flour with baking powder and add to bowl, stir and fill into baking dish. Bake for around forty-five minutes at 180 degrees Celsius. A toothpick inserted in centre should come out clean.

Mix icing sugar with a bit of water and spread over warm cake.

ENCHANTING AROMA OF CINNAMON

Egyptians used cinnamon for embalming because it destroys fungi and bacteria. Until 1833, the tree used to grow only in Ceylon (Sri Lanka). Cinnamon gets its scent and flavour from a chemical compound called cinnamaldehyde. Just smelling cinnamon boosts memory and concentration. Studies show people with type 2 diabetes can decrease blood sugar and cholesterol levels by consuming one gram of cinnamon a day. A glass of hot water with a tablespoon cinnamon and honey can stop medication-resistant yeast infections and joint pain. If you take cinnamon regularly, use the one from Sri Lanka, not the Indian variety, 'cassia cinnamon'. Cassia contains coumarin, which damages the liver.

TRUST YOUR JUDGEMENT

Over the years, I have developed a few strong opinions. When I was young, I felt I knew nothing. I still feel that I know little about the mysteries of life. I consider this a good thing because it keeps my mind open. I don't want to get stuck in a fixed frame of attitudes.

Regarding food, I have done my homework in many ways and I feel entitled to opinions. I follow with interest what scientists discover all over the world. I learn and keep myself informed but that does not mean I believe everything. Over the years, we have listened to a lot of advice from experts that turned out to be wrong. We were not supposed to eat many eggs, coconuts were considered unhealthy because of the saturated fat content, and butter was said to contribute to high levels of cholesterol.

In the end, I trust myself. I can assure you that a diet with plenty of prebiotics and probiotics makes your digestion work, and improves your mood. Please don't take anything you read about food as a law written in stone. Diets and experts contradict each other; you will find people swearing on each and every one of them.

Trust your judgement. Don't eat food just because somebody recommends it. Watch your body and how it reacts to what you eat. Don't allow anything into your mouth that does not taste right. When something is delicious, it makes you happy for a little while – and that is healthy, no matter what.

PART 2

COMFORT FOOD

'Nothing would be more tiresome than eating
and drinking if God had not made them a
pleasure as well as a necessity'

VOLTAIRE, FRENCH WRITER

CHAPTER 5

SAVOURY SUCCULENCE

ometimes I wish I could be a child again. I fondly remember the days when life was simple. I did not have to worry about running my household, paying bills and keeping my men well-fed and reasonably content. As a child, I did not dream about making millions of dollars. My favourite chocolate cake could send me to heaven. It may not be the most sophisticated way to achieve pleasure, but it works.

I believe we should harvest pleasure whenever possible. Comfort food guarantees instant gratification. As long as you enjoy your indulgence, it works. Stuffing things into your mouth to fill a hole in your heart does not count. Most of us have been there and done that, once in a while. When you constantly seek solace in food, you are ready for psychotherapy.

Our lives should not revolve around seeking pleasure only. But we all need a little something to take the edge off our daily troubles. Everybody has to deal with problems. Enlightened persons may float in ecstatic aloofness above the mass of more or less miserable mortals. I don't think these blessed ones read my humble cookbook. I assume that you, dear reader, struggle your way through life as I do.

I agree with Dr Lavinia Rodriguez, an expert in weight management. She states that the psychological value of comfort food is immense. If we deny ourselves the foods that make us happy, our minds and bodies will crave for them. We don't need to sacrifice our favourite foods to remain healthy and slim. We just have to balance how much and how often we eat them.

There is a big difference between comfort and junk food. Comfort food is cooked at home with fresh ingredients. Ample amounts of butter and cream pamper your palate and your mind. That's why comfort food is generally rich in calories. That does not make it an unhealthy pleasure. Remember to choose fat that our bodies can absorb. I stick to cold-pressed olive oil, coconut oil, butter and ghee.

Liberate yourself from nutrition experts that tell you to eat only low fat food. Experts tend to be wrong. Trust your taste buds and feel free to enjoy. Comfort foods delight us instantly, a simple pleasure when your mind benefits from the sensations of your palate. Thank God for bacon, chocolate and cream.

MELTDOWN OF WILL POWER

Psychotherapy helped me at the age of thirty to overcome eating disorders. My stint with anorexia nervosa had ended long before. My healthy core overpowered my self-destructive urges during a holiday at the Côte d'Azur.

tabbouleh

chicken liver pâté

Brussels sprouts

guacamole

chicken-pesto rolls

surprise burgers

rainbow frittata

quinoa pie

pasta with walnut sauce

Mexican beans and
brown rice

jumbo crabs

mussels alla marinara

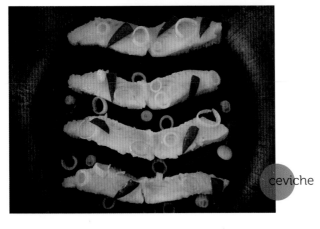

ceviche

seafood risotto

garlic prawns

gigantes

Indianized fasolada

fish with beurre blanc

zwiebelkuchen

falafel

hummus

tzatziki

key lime pie

qubani ka meetha

panna cotta

profiteroles

Nineteen years old, I had just completed high school. The Abitur, comparable to the baccalaureate, enabled me to visit any German university. To celebrate, I had travelled to the Côte d'Azur with some classmates. Because we had not enough money for a hotel, we pitched our tents at a campsite close to Fréjus. We swam in the sea, bathed in the sun and danced the night away. Free at last, I lost control over my body. Starving seemed somehow pointless.

The supermarket at the campsite sold heavenly pastries. Fluffy, crunchy puff pastry filled with silky crème pâtissière: I just could not resist. The wine that we drank for lunch and dinner helped to dissolve all self-control. I felt liberated, like a ton of weight had lifted. I was not afraid of becoming fat any more.

On the last evening, we watched the sunset on the beach. Suddenly, I felt my heart opening. I felt happy. I felt the beauty of the world, the beauty of life. I decided to leave fear behind, to live life to the fullest. This resolve stayed with me for a long time after the sun had set. I followed this decision, no regrets.

I returned from this holiday five kilograms heavier. We all thought I had snapped out of a passing mood. While I prepared to leave home for university, I kept reading my cookbooks. I was ready for yummy stuff – and I started with pasta carbonara. I begin the recipes for comfort food with the Indianised version.

51 PASTA WITH BACON AND CREAM

This is my recipe for instant comfort food. You can light the pot with pasta water. While the water comes to a boil and you cook the pasta, your sauce will be ready. Many words have been written about bacon, cured meat from the belly of pigs, the number one ingredient for non-vegetarians.

For the sauce, you have to render the fat: slowly fry the bacon over medium heat until the fat turns into oil and the meaty bits crisp up.

INGREDIENTS

(Serves 4)

- 1 packet Italian pasta (500 gm)
- 1 packet cream (200 ml)
- 1 packet smoked bacon (200 gm)
- Salt
- Freshly ground pepper
- Parmigiano or grana cheese

☞ TIP: You can use more bacon if you want, but not less.

METHOD

Cut bacon into small pieces and fry until crispy. Save some crispy bacon bits for garnishing.

Fill a pot with water for pasta. When water is boiling, add two tablespoons of salt. Add pasta, stir and cook for as many minutes as indicated on the packet. Never put a lid on a pot with boiling pasta.

Shortly before pasta is ready, mix bacon with cream and simmer for 1 minute. Take four to six tablespoons of pasta water and stir into sauce to make coating of pasta easier. Drain pasta and mix with sauce.

Sprinkle crispy bacon over pasta and grind lots of black pepper over it. Serve immediately with grated parmigiano or grana cheese.

TASTY BACON: A SPECIAL TREAT

Meat-lovers adore the aroma of sizzling bacon.

But there is a big but: bacon is not a healthy food. Meat from the abdomen of the pig is cured with nitrites, which give bacon its reddish colour. During frying, nitrites are transformed into cancer-causing nitrosamines.

I believe, when you enjoy a wholesome diet, your body can take some bacon but not on a daily basis. Enjoy your bacon; just ensure it remains a special treat.

INDULGE YOURSELF

After I had given up starving, I faced another kind of eating disorder: binge eating. Shortly after my return from the holidays in France, I left my parents' home to study in Erlangen, only sixty kilometres away from Ansbach. I rented a tiny room in an apartment let to students.

From the outside, I lived like any other student. I attended lessons and tried to get to know fellow students. Alone, I often fell into a black hole and stuffed myself with food. I felt completely helpless during these attacks.

A recent study has shown that eating comfort food can decrease feelings of loneliness. Even only thinking or writing about favourite foods furthers emotional well-being. The only condition to make comfort food work is to enjoy it wholeheartedly. Savour every bite and don't feel guilty.

Comfort food remains an individual affair. All cultures have customs around special food items and every family develops its own favourites. What is heaven for one person might be hell for another. However, some things are globally appreciated. When you search for most popular comfort food, you find one item all over the world: lasagne (or lasagna). A proper lasagne lives from the combination of tasty ragout, masses of béchamel sauce, and a crunchy crust of melted cheese. Good lasagne leaves you with a satisfied feeling.

52 LASAGNE

You can prepare lasagne some hours in advance, but it must be served shortly after baking. If you are in a hurry, you can use readymade ragout sauce, tomato sauce with minced meat, one essential in my freezer. I always cook a big pot and freeze portions.

Be careful when you buy pasta sheets for lasagne. Often they are only packed in cardboard leading to mould in the humid Indian climate.

For a vegetarian version, replace the ragout with tomato sauce and 400 grams white button mushrooms. Clean and slice the mushrooms and use them between the layers of pasta sheets on top of the tomato sauce.

INGREDIENTS

(Serves 8)

- 12 lasagne sheets (the non-cook variety)
- 1 litre milk
- 600 gm mozzarella cheese
- 100 gm butter
- ½ cup flour
- ½ kg minced beef
- 3 onions
- 1 big carrot
- 3 big cloves garlic
- 1 stick celery
- 2 packets of tomato puree (200 ml each)
- 5 tbsp olive oil
- Salt
- Pepper
- Butter to grease the baking dish

METHOD

Clean and cut onions. Heat olive oil in a pan. Fry minced meat on all sides, add onions and keep frying until onions brown a bit. Add grated carrots, tomato puree and crushed garlic. Cover with water and simmer over a low flame for at least one hour. You can add a dash of red wine and more water if needed. Season with salt and pepper. It should not be liquidy but creamy.

Grate mozzarella cheese. Prepare béchamel sauce by melting the butter, adding the flour in one go and then stirring vigorously to avoid clumps.

Then incorporate the milk gradually. Add about one cup of milk to the roux while stirring. This will make the roux seize up and turn into a thick cream. Keep adding the milk cup by cup while stirring.

Gradually, the roux will loosen up. Now you need to bring the béchamel gently to a simmer. After one or two minutes of simmering, the sauce should thicken. At this point, adjust the seasoning. You have to use the béchamel sauce as quickly as possible. As soon as it cools down, a skin will form over the sauce. You can dissolve this skin several times by stirring it, but you want to avoid letting the sauce cool down too much.

Butter bottom and sides of a baking dish (13×9 inches or 32×22 centimetres).

Place ragout, béchamel sauce and grated mozzarella next to baking dish. Put a layer of pasta sheets into dish. Leave some place around sheets because they double in size during baking. Sprinkle sheets with mozzarella. Spread one-third of your ragout sauce over sheets, sprinkle with mozzarella and top with béchamel sauce. Continue layering in this way and finish with béchamel sauce. Sprinkle mozzarella over béchamel sauce.

Bake lasagne at 200 degrees Celsius for thirty minutes. The cheese should form a golden crust.

MOZZARELLA FOR LACTOSE INTOLERANCE

Mozzarella is the cheese for persons with lactose intolerance.

Mozzarella is made with a fast process of fermentation and washed in plenty of hot water that removes lactose residue.

Fresh mozzarella should be eaten as quickly as possible, preferably on the day of the production. If you cook with it, you can take the sealed varieties with long shelf life. Like all dairy products, mozzarella contains a lot of calcium, vitamin D and B.

INDIVIDUAL COMFORT FOOD

The selection of recipes in this book has taken place in a highly subjective manner. Yours truly represents the most important influence although everybody who crossed my way had to endure the question: 'What is your favourite food?'

My late father had handed down the following recipe for Zwiebelkuchen. He used to prepare it regularly. Every year, we visited our relatives in Alsace who had a vineyard. After returning home with a trunk full of fresh wine, my father prepared Zwiebelkuchen and we tasted the different wines. I call it Zwiebelkuchen because the English translation, 'onion cake', does not fit the subject. I include this highly individualistic choice of comfort food recipe because it hits the spot – and my guests agree.

53 ZWIEBELKUCHEN

Zwiebelkuchen comes from Swabia in south Germany. Swabia shares a long border with France and Switzerland. Swabia's citizens are known for careful handling of money. Stuttgart is the capital of Swabia and the richest German town, and seat of Mercedes Benz and Porsche, offers wonderful museums.

Like the cars, the cuisine is beautiful, solid and rich. Zwiebelkuchen is always served with wine.

INGREDIENTS

(Serves 6)

- 2½ cups flour
- 1 packet dry yeast
- 100 ml milk
- 100 gm butter
- ¾ kg onions
- 100 gm bacon
- 125 ml cream
- 2 eggs
- 2 egg yolks
- 2 tbsp sugar
- Salt
- Pepper
- Butter to grease a cookie sheet

☞ TIP: For a vegetarian version, substitute the bacon with two tablespoons cumin seeds. If you want some zing in your Zwiebelkuchen, chop some green chillies and mix it with the onions while frying.

METHOD

Mix dry yeast with 100 millilitres water and two tablespoons sugar. Place flour in a bowl and make a hole in middle. When dissolved yeast starts to bubble, pour it into this hole and cover with flour.

When flour shows cracks, add fifty grams butter, eggs, milk and one teaspoon salt. Knead with your hands to obtain elastic dough. You might need to add more water. Grease a cookie sheet with butter. Roll out dough to cover sheet.

While dough is rising, peel and slice onions. Chop bacon. Fry bacon in a pan until it renders fat. Add remaining butter and onions. Fry until onions turn translucent. Add half a cup of water. Cook onions until soft, but not brown. Combine cream with egg yolks; mix with onions and season with salt and pepper.

Cover yeast dough with onions and bake at 200 degrees Celsius for about half an hour. Serve warm.

CREAMY DELICIOUSNESS

Cream contains most of the fatty parts of milk. Although it is high in fat, it delivers the saturated kinds of fat our bodies need and can absorb easily. Cream delivers a healthy amount of minerals too, with calcium topping the list, followed by potassium, phosphorus and magnesium. As with everything rich in calories, the following also applies to cream: A little goes a long way.

CRISPY, CHEWY, CREAMY

Texture is as important as flavour. Food can look, smell and taste great, but when it feels unfamiliar to our hands, tongue and palate, it can be repulsive. Grainy mousse au chocolate or soggy profiteroles do not hit the spot. I love crispy-crunchy together with creamy. Crunchy garlic bread with creamy pâté or ice cream with toasted almonds makes me happy. Any kind of fat delivers a creamy sensation in the mouth. That's why most comfort foods share one trait: high levels of fat and calories.

The palate, the roof of the mouth, is extremely sensitive. They can detect ice grains forty microns (1/25 of a millimetre) small. Our taste buds only distinguish between salty, sweet, sour and bitter. The food industry employs experts of texture; the science of food structure even has a name, food rheology. The three most popular textures are crispy, creamy and chewy.

Malcolm Bourne from Cornell University writes in his book *Food Texture and Viscosity* that we have an ingrained need to chew. Gnawing improves the blood flow to the brain, preventing dementia.

I need crunch in many dishes. Pizza does not deliver without crunchy crust. Today, I can crank out several pizzas without breaking into sweat. In Germany we have a saying: 'Exercise makes the master.' This is especially true when it comes to cooking. The more often you repeat a recipe, the easier it seems. That does not mean disasters can be avoided – too much can go wrong at any given moment.

I started making pizza because I cannot stand the commercial varieties. For a decent amount of cheese you have to order double and the dough tastes like the cardboard it is delivered on, not to mention the bill that qualifies pizza as luxury food.

54 HOMEMADE PIZZA

My pizza has little to do with the stuff delivered on scooter. I make the dough from scratch with whole wheat flour. My pizza resembles the Italian kind, a thin crust with loads of cheese. Our favourite topping is an anchovy here and there, about half a tin for a pizza.

Many times, I stick to vegetarian toppings like mushrooms or bell pepper. Italian oregano is a must for proper taste. I always make at least five pizzas. If there are no friends around, we eat two pizzas for dinner. The rest I keep in the fridge and heat them before serving.

INGREDIENTS

(Makes 5)

- 750 gm whole wheat flour
- 2 packets dry yeast
- 3 packets tomato puree (200 ml each)
- 5 packets mozzarella cheese (200 gm each)
- Any kind of topping you like
- Extra virgin olive oil
- Dried oregano
- Salt
- Water

METHOD

Dissolve yeast in warm water and two tablespoons sugar. Place flour into a big bowl and make a hole in centre. When yeast starts to bubble, pour it into this hole. Cover with flour. When you see cracks in flour, mix yeast with flour, water and one tablespoon salt. You need around half a litre of water to obtain elastic dough.

Let rise for one hour. Dough should double in size. Divide dough into five equal pieces, roll into balls and dust with flour.

Grate cheese; I use a blender. Cut toppings. Place tomato puree into a bowl and mix with one-teaspoon salt.

Place all ingredients – grated cheese, olive oil, tomato puree, oregano and toppings – within easy reach of your work surface. Preheat oven to 250 degrees Celsius.

Spread oil over a cookie sheet or stainless steel plate. Roll a ball of dough as thinly as possible and place it on plate. Brush olive oil evenly over dough; cover with a thin layer of tomato puree and lots of cheese. Sprinkle pizza with oregano and add toppings of your choice.

Bake pizza until dough is crunchy and cheese forms a golden crust.

THE POTENT LEAVES OF OREGANO

The tiny leaves of the oregano shrub give their unique flavour to pizza and a lot of other Mediterranean dishes. Recent studies have shown that one tablespoon of fresh oregano has more than forty times the antioxidant power of apples. This herb contains volatile oils that inhibit the growth of many kinds of bacteria. One study reports that oregano treats the common amoeba giardia more effectively than a prescription drug.

☞ **TIP:** Packed mozzarella cheese works well for pizza. If you find fresh mozzarella, go for it and forget about the price: it tastes much better.

MAKE ROOM FOR PLEASURE

When eating disorders held me in their grip, I could not enjoy food. Food was the enemy, an almost mystic opponent. While starving myself I revelled in the illusion that I had defeated this enemy. When anorexia changed into binge eating I could not deny the fact that I was screwed up. Something was wrong with me. But I did not know how to escape.

For years I led a double existence – also during my apprenticeship at the newspaper. My public persona showed a cheerful young woman, a little on the chubby side. My private persona was a mess. Alone I starved or stuffed myself. In the beginning I tried to purge food by sticking a finger into my mouth, but my gag reflex did not work well. My binge eating did not lead to dramatic weight gain. I never weighed more than sixty-seven kilograms. That did not diminish my anguish.

Thanks to my eating disorders, I have amassed a wealth of knowledge based on experience, not theory. I know that restrictive diets cannot work. I don't agree with nutritionists that deny us our favourite meals. Food is not the enemy, even when our favourite meal is a dietary nightmare. Once in a while our bodies can handle it.

I found balance with my first husband. After I met him, my eating disorders disappeared. I have no idea why, but falling in love and Greek food saved me from binge eating.

While living in Greece, my weight hovered around fifty-five kilograms, although Greeks use tons of olive oil. Greeks love fried potatoes, a classic comfort food all over the world. Today, most of these tubers end up as French fries or crisps in fast food joints.

55 ULTIMATE FRIED POTATOES

I own a cookbook by Eliza Acton with the title *Modern Cookery*, published in 1845. She describes three different ways of boiling potatoes. Her staggering variety of potato recipes does not include French fries. I have studied the methods recommended by famous chefs. Heston Blumenthal's guide to the perfect French fries involves three steps, including a stop in the freezer.

I don't mind hard work but there is a limit to what I am willing to do. When I cook, I clean afterwards. Using three different pots makes me reluctant to follow a recipe. Famous chefs like Heston Blumenthal command an army of kitchen helpers. I don't doubt that the results are outstanding but I want pleasures simple to execute.

That's where my ultimate fried potatoes come into play. It is so easy that everybody can do it. I call my version the ultimate fried potatoes because it delivers crunch without the pains of double or triple frying. I boil my potatoes first until almost done. During frying in oil they develop a golden crust that reveals a satiny smoothness.

INGREDIENTS

(Serves 4)

- 1 kg potatoes
- Oil for deep-frying
- Salt

☞ **TIP:** Sprinkle the fried potatoes with freshly grated pepper and fresh, chopped herbs like parsley or thyme.

METHOD

Peel potatoes and cut them into pieces of equal size.

Place potatoes into a pressure cooker; add two centimetres of water and two teaspoons of salt. Cook for five to ten minutes on low flame after first whistle until almost done. Drain them.

Heat oil in a frying pan and add potatoes. Fry until golden brown on all sides. This takes some time. Drain excess fat on kitchen towels and serve immediately.

FRIED POTATOES, OH SO YUMMY

Everybody loves fried potatoes because they deliver everything we desire from comfort food. Their crunchy outside reveals a soft interior, ticking the boxes when it comes to texture. Even elderly people can enjoy chewing French fries or a version of this recipe, because their crunch easily gives way to satiny starch, calming the mind. The saltiness of fried potatoes adds mouth appeal. The high amount of fat supplies the nice feeling of roundness in the belly that all comfort foods provide. French fries are a special treat that can bulk up your hips if you eat them daily.

SOFTEN THE BLOWS OF LIFE

Opinions about mashed potatoes are divided: people love or hate them. My men belong to the second category; I love mashed potatoes. Mashed potatoes render life soft for a little while – no conflict, no hard edges. When I have to digest a blow, I turn to mashed potatoes. A little gravy or fried eggs turn them into a complete meal. If you need mashed potatoes, chances are you feel bruised, and not ready for a lot of cooking.

56 MASHED POTATOES

Again, Heston Blumenthal's way of preparing mashed potatoes is way too complicated for me. I admire his passion and his knowledge of molecular gastronomy though. Heston simmers his potatoes for half an hour in salt water at seventy-two degrees. Then he rinses and boils, dries and infuses milk with potato peels before finally mashing them, pushing the mash through a sieve and adding an indecent amount of butter. Give me a break! Exactly seventy-two degrees!

Heston's directions work well for hobby cooks. Grudgingly, I have to admit that my recipe might not result in the best mashed potatoes, but they do the job and you don't have to watch a pot for half an hour.

INGREDIENTS

(Serves 6)

- 1 kg starchy potatoes
- 300 ml milk (you might need a bit more)
- 150 gm butter
- Salt
- Pepper
- Nutmeg

METHOD

You need potato pieces of equal size so they cook evenly. You need to cook them just right, not too long and not too short. You should not overwork potatoes during mashing; otherwise starch might turn gluey. You need to warm up milk and butter so they mix easily with mashed potatoes.

A potato masher and a fine sieve are essential. I use a potato ricer. It forces potatoes through small holes and delivers a more uniform result than a masher.

Peel potatoes and cut into pieces. I use a pressure cooker to boil them. Add about two centimetres of water and two teaspoons of salt. Cook for ten minutes on low flame after first whistle.

Drain and let cool down. You need dry potatoes that are not too hot. Heat milk with butter and stir.

Mash potatoes in a bowl, add warm milk and stir carefully with a big spoon. Season with salt and pepper and/or a bit of grated nutmeg. Push through a finely meshed sieve for optimum results.

POTATO: SUPERIOR TO IMAGE

The potato is a tuber – part of an underground stem that nourishes the leaves of the plant. The effect of potatoes on our bodies largely depends on the way of cooking. Baked in the oven, steamed or boiled, it offers a lot of nutrients for our health. Potatoes contain plenty of vitamin C and B6, copper, potassium, manganese, and dietary fibre.

A cup of baked potato supplies more than 26 per cent of the daily intake of vitamin B6. This alone makes the potato a valuable asset in the kitchen. Vitamin B6 is involved in more than 100 enzymatic reactions everywhere in the human body. Many proteins and parts of the DNA require vitamin B6. This vitamin is of vital importance for our nervous system and the performance of our brain cells. It also helps to break down glycogen in muscle cells and the liver, providing energy when needed.

FORGIVE AND FORGET

Nigella Lawson has inspired the following recipe. Although she has come under public scrutiny, I still love watching her shows. I don't know if she uses drugs and I don't need to know. There is a lot of truth to be found in the Bible: 'Do not judge, and you will not be judged. Forgive, and you will be forgiven.' I guess we all need to be forgiven sometimes.

Nigella uses a lot of ingredients that you cannot find in India but she keeps giving me ideas. I use local ingredients whenever I can. Shipping food around the world is responsible for tons of greenhouse gases, causing global warming.

Locally grown chicken can be found everywhere and they are easy to prepare. Fried chicken pieces from restaurants taste nice, but it feels like lead in my stomach. Because my son loves friend chicken, I do a home-cooked version.

57 CRISPY CHICKEN DRUMSTICKS

Nigella marinates her chicken overnight in milk and then cooks it in the milk. I consider this a waste. I use salt water with great results. Poaching the chicken before frying makes sure that it is cooked all the way through. I love sweet chilli sauce together with the crispy drumsticks, but any dipping sauce will do.

INGREDIENTS

(Serves 4)

- 12 chicken drumsticks (around 1 kg)
- 3 eggs
- 2 cups flour
- Salt
- Red chilli powder
- White pepper
- Oil or ghee for deep-frying

FOR CHILLI SAUCE

(Makes 500 ml)

- 🌶 20 red Thai chillies
- 🌶 4 big cloves garlic
- 🌶 1 cup castor sugar
- 🌶 5 tbsp white wine vinegar
- 🌶 Salt

☞ **TIP:** You can use any flavours you like for the chicken. You can do this recipe also with chicken breasts. Cut them into bite-sized pieces after poaching.

METHOD

Finely chop chillies for chilli sauce. Bring sugar with two cups of water to a boil; add chillies, garlic, one tablespoon salt and vinegar. Stir and simmer for fifteen minutes. Let it cool down and adjust seasoning.

Wash and clean drumsticks. Bring a pot of water to a boil. Add two tablespoons salt and immerse drumsticks. Simmer for twenty minutes. Let drumsticks cool down. Break eggs into a deep plate and add one tablespoon salt, two tablespoons chilli powder and one tablespoon ground pepper.

Place one cup of flour into a plastic bag with a zip. Add chicken legs one by one and shake around to coat evenly with flour. Roll each drumstick in beaten egg and coat again with flour. Refill flour in plastic bag when needed.

Heat enough oil, at least half a litre, in a wok or a deep fryer. I have started using ghee for deep-frying because it is healthier than most vegetable oils. The fat is hot enough when a piece of bread browns in one minute. Fry chicken drumsticks until golden brown and serve immediately with sauce.

UNIVERSAL CURE FROM THE KITCHEN

Chicken soup has cured millions of dripping noses, fevers and flu attacks. Greek cuisine healed my soul, and my favourite chicken soup comes from there. It carries the name 'kotosoupa avgolemono', translated literally, chicken soup egg lemon.

Every mother needs to know how to cook chicken soup. My teenage son still asks for it when he feels under the weather. Every country has its own peculiar way of making chicken soup. Germans, ever so waste conscious, use the poor old hens that don't lay enough eggs any more. Poor things, all their lives they lay eggs and when they don't produce enough any more, they land in the soup pot.

A German chicken soup is straightforward, with carrots, onions and celery. Mexican chicken soups come with a red broth, coloured by chillies and tomatoes while Asian chicken soups use bok choy, spring onions and shitake mushrooms. Jewish people serve matzo balls in chicken soups.

58 CHICKEN SOUP

'Avgolemono' describes the way of thickening the soup. Eggs and lemon juice are stirred together and incorporated into the liquid. This adds zing and a light yellow, creamy consistency. Eggs curdle easily, so you need to respect some rules. Have your eggs at room temperature. Let the soup cool down before incorporating the egg-lemon mixture. Gradually add enough warm soup to the egg-lemon mixture to reach roughly the same temperature as the soup in the pot. Don't boil the soup after adding eggs.

INGREDIENTS

(Serves 4)

- 🍗 1 kg chicken
- 🍗 1 onion
- 🍗 2 carrots
- 🍗 1 celery stick
- 🍗 2 cloves garlic
- 🍗 ¾ cup rice
- 🍗 2 eggs
- 🍗 4 tbsp lemon or lime juice
- 🍗 Salt
- 🍗 Pepper

☞ **TIP:** You can add more or less lemon juice. If you want zing, boil fresh chillies with the chicken.

METHOD

Remove eggs and lemons from fridge. Clean and wash chicken. Cut it into four pieces that makes it easier to handle. Place into a big pot and cover with water.

Clean and roughly chop vegetables and add to pot. Close with a lid and bring it to a boil. Simmer chicken for at least one hour. Remove any scum that collects on surface. Chicken is done when meat comes away from bones.

Place chicken on a plate and strain soup. You should have around one litre; if not, add water. Bring soup to a boil, add rice and cook until done. Remove meat from bones and cut into pieces. Season soup with salt and pepper. Switch off flame.

Crack eggs into a bowl. Add lemon juice and whisk. Add one tablespoon of soup at a time and stir. When temperature of egg mixture equals that of soup, combine with soup. Add meat and serve immediately.

CHICKEN SOUP, THE GOODNESS OF BONE BROTH

To make it short: Probably the biggest advantage of chicken soup is its reputation to cure everything from broken bones to heavy colds. A chicken soup makes us feel good, remembering childhood days when our mothers made it for us as a way of expressing their love. Chicken soup delivers the goodness of a homemade bone broth. That means, it has plenty of calcium and other minerals found in bones. Chicken soup contains a protein called cysteine that thins the mucus in the lungs. It also delivers plenty of fluids, always a good thing when we are sick.

GARLIC OVERDOSE

One of my weirdest experiences was a garlic overdose. In 1989 I lived with my Greek husband in Regensburg. One day I made Tzatziki for a potluck party, with fresh garlic from my favourite vegetable shop run by a Turkish man in one of the medieval streets.

The garlic smelled delicious and I used a full head for one kilogram of rich, Greek yoghurt. Before the party, my stomach kept grumbling and I kept dipping baguette into my tzatziki. After some drinks I might have nibbled again at the tzatziki. In the wee hours of the morning, I woke up with a bloated belly. I kept burping – each time the taste of fresh garlic rose from my belly. Nauseating! This went on for a full day. I could only stay in bed, burping helplessly. Needless to say, I have learnt my lesson.

59 TZATZIKI

The Greek dish tzatziki is the European equivalent of 'raita'. The freshness of cucumber mingles with thick curd scented with garlic. You need rich yoghurt for this dip. I always use homemade hung curd, as described in the chapter about 'Kitchen Must-Haves'. I call this the best tzatziki in India, because I have never tasted a better one here. Please forgive my boasting.

INGREDIENTS

(Serves 8)

- 2½ cups hung curd
- 4 tablespoons olive oil
- 2 tablespoons vinegar
- 3 medium-sized cucumbers

- 5 big cloves garlic
- Salt
- Pepper

☞ **TIP:** If you like zing in your tzatziki, add chopped fresh green chillies.

METHOD

Peel and deseed cucumbers, then grate them. Place into sieve. Lightly salt and drain them for half an hour. Get rid of as much water as you can. Crush garlic.

Mix curd with cucumbers, garlic, olive oil and vinegar. Add salt and pepper according to taste and serve chilled.

CURD KEEPS YOU HEALTHY FROM INSIDE

Millions of active bacteria in curd offer many benefits. Curd is a better source of calcium than milk, because we digest it easier. Eating yoghurt regularly helps with yeast infections and strengthens the immune system. Eating lots of live active yoghurt keeps even ulcer-causing bacteria under control.

When buying curd, make sure it is fresh, or make it yourself. Simply mix one litre of milk with two tablespoons of yoghurt. Keep overnight at a warm place.

IS COMFORT FOOD A MYTH?

Sometimes I get mad when I read ignorant and shallow stuff. An article from Tom Jacobs published on the Pacific Standard website carries the headline 'Comfort food is a myth'. A team at the University of Minnesota showed sad movies to the participants of a test to investigate the effect of comfort food. After the movie, some participants received their favourite comfort foods, some had to eat so-called neutral foods, and some unlucky ones got nothing. Then they had to fill out a questionnaire to determine their mood change. The result: It did not matter if people ate or not; after a short while their mood bounced back.

The researchers, led by psychologist Tracy Mann, concluded: 'Removing an excuse for eating a high-calorie or high-fat food may help people develop and maintain healthier eating habits, and may lead them to focus on other, food-free methods of improving their mood.' The author of the article even wrote: 'We've lost another rationalisation for eating junk food.'

I wholeheartedly disagree. I don't doubt that the average person recovers quickly after a mildly disconcerting experience like watching a sad movie. Filling questionnaires seems a crude way of assessing one's state of mind. I think measuring brain waves – like the researchers at the University of Leuven in Belgium did – is a more objective way of detecting effects on the brain. Remember, the scientists in Belgium found that fatty food boosts our mood.

I completely disagree also with Tom Jacobs. The author equals comfort with junk food. One thing has nothing to do with the other. Comfort food is cooked at home using fresh ingredients. The result may be high in calories but free of chemicals used by the food industry. Junk food is the output of a fast food diner or a food factory – loaded with additives for the purpose of making money. Obesity is not caused by comfort food but by food additives and eating disorders.

The following recipe is my tribute to the country that has allowed me to make a home for my family. I don't think you can find a beach shack in Goa that does not offer the typical Goan prawn curry.

60 GOAN PRAWN CURRY

Once in a while, I cook Goan prawn curry. Preparing curry remains a culinary adventure for me, a task that I do not perform in India but in Europe. Whenever I invite my European relatives and friends to our homes in Bavaria or Milano, I try to cook something special.

Some of the ingredients I take with me from Goa, mainly spices like pepper corns, coriander and cumin seeds. The first time I made this recipe in Bavaria, I showed restraint with chillies but my Bavarian friends had tears in their eyes, although they ate the curry bravely with gusto.

Curries have conquered the world. The British have adopted curries like few other nations. Two hundred years ago, an Indian migrant named Dean Mahomed opened Britain's first curry house. Nowadays most people know that a proper curry has little to do with the powder that shares its name. How you make your prawn curry depends upon your preferences. I use big prawns and I don't cook them as long as a Goan housewife would do. For my taste, prawns should only change their colour during a gentle simmer. When you boil prawns for five minutes, they turn hard and lose a lot of volume.

INGREDIENTS

(Serves 4)

- 500 gm cleaned tiger prawns
- 4 tbsp olive oil
- 3 tbsp tamarind pulp
- 1 small onion
- 5 green chillies
- 10 curry leaves
- 2 cups coconut milk
- Salt
- Fresh coriander to garnish

FOR THE PASTE

- 5 big garlic cloves
- 1 tsp coriander seeds
- ½ tsp cumin seeds
- 10 dry red chillies
- 10 peppercorns
- 1 small, chopped onion
- 1 tbsp turmeric powder
- 1 cup fresh grated coconut
- 1 cup water

FOR THE RICE

- 500 grams Basmati rice
- 5 green cardamom pods
- 8 cloves
- 1 stick cinnamon

METHOD

Wash and devein prawns: slit along backside and remove dark strings. Sprinkle with salt and keep aside.

Crush garlic. Place ingredients for paste into a grinder. Old-fashioned housewives use a masala stone. A modern high-power grinder will do. A normal blender is not strong enough. I grind ingredients in a mortar and pestle and mix paste with water. You should obtain a smooth paste.

Crush cardamom pods for rice to release aroma. Place rice with double its volume of water, spices and salt into a pot. Cover with lid and bring to a boil. Turn down heat and simmer until rice has absorbed water. Fluff it with a fork before serving.

Clean and chop onion for curry. Heat oil in a pan. Add curry leaves and onion and fry for four to five minutes until onion softens. Crush chillies with a big knife. Add paste, tamarind pulp and chillies and fry for two to three minutes. Add coconut milk and stir until combined well. Add prawns and simmer curry gently until the prawns have changed colour, not longer than two or three minutes.

Sprinkle fresh, chopped coriander leaves over curry and serve immediately.

THE POWERFUL PODS OF CARDAMOM

Cardamom is widely used in Indian cooking for good reason. These spice pods not only freshen the breath, they also improve our health in many ways. Cardamom is one of the most beneficial spices for digestion. It speeds up the metabolism because it increases the flow of saliva. It also reduces inflammation of the stomach lining and fights heartburn and feelings of nausea. Furthermore, cardamom improves the blood flow to the lungs, relieving respiratory illness like asthma. The minerals in cardamom help to regulate the heartbeat. Last, but not least, it has the reputation of being a strong aphrodisiac.

INDIA ON A PLATE

When I rode my Enfield Bullet through India, I almost got killed on the highways many times. Trucks and jeeps swerved dangerously close. I fell into icy rivers and lost control on stony dirt roads. The experience of near-death changed me. Every survivor knows that he or she is lucky to be alive, that we should savour the moment.

On the road, I used to stop for dal makhani with rotis at dhabas along the highways. This dish is India on a plate for me. When the perfect symphony of spices of dal mingles with rotis, you easily forget that your arms hurt and your skin is black from exhaust fumes.

61 DAL MAKHANI WITH CHAPATIS

Roti or chapati dough needs plenty of muscle. As a German, I love everything resembling bread. When I cook this dal, I always make double – for eight servings. It keeps well in the fridge. Some people say it tastes better when you warm it up. You can also freeze it.

INGREDIENTS

(Serves 4)

- 1 cup whole black lentils (sabut urad)
- 2 tbsp red kidney beans (rajma beans)
- 3 tbsp oil
- 3 tbsp (or a bit more) butter
- 1 large onion
- 6 cloves garlic
- 1 packet (200 ml) tomato puree
- 2 green chillies
- ½ cup (100 ml) cream
- 1 tsp red chilli powder
- 2 inch piece of ginger
- 1 tsp cumin seeds
- 1 tsp garam masala
- ¼ tsp turmeric powder
- 2 cloves
- 1 inch cinnamon stick
- 3 green cardamom pods

FOR 12 CHAPATIS

- 2 cups whole wheat flour
- 2 tsp oil
- 1 tbsp salt
- Water

METHOD

Clean and soak lentils and kidney beans overnight. Drain,

rinse and place into a pressure cooker. Add a pinch of salt and cover with water. Pressure cook for half an hour on low flame after first whistle.

For chapati dough, place flour with salt into a bowl. Warm up oil for twenty seconds in microwave. Add to flour and mix everything, then add one cup of water. Knead dough with fingers. Gradually add small quantities of water until you obtain smooth dough. Knead for at least five minutes. Cover dough with wet tea towel and let it rest for one hour.

Skin and grate ginger. You can also use one tablespoon of ginger paste. Crush garlic. Heat butter and oil in a deep pan. Add cumin seeds. When they crackle, add green chillies, cinnamon, cloves, crushed cardamom pods and chopped onion.

Fry while stirring constantly. When onions have turned golden, add ginger, garlic, chilli and turmeric powder and tomato puree. Cook over medium heat until oil appears on top. Add legumes and a bit of water if necessary and simmer for fifteen minutes. Finally add cream and season with salt. Serve with a dollop of cream and sprinkle some coriander leaves.

To make chapatis, divide the dough into twelve equal pieces. Roll into circles on a surface covered with flour. Heat a non-stick pan and heat chapatis over high flame on both sides.

GARAM MASALA, THE MAGIC SPICE MIXTURE

Although garam masala comes in many variations, some ingredients for this spice mix are essential and deliver amazing health benefits for our bodies. The combination of pepper, cloves, cinnamon and cardamom lowers cholesterol levels and improves the memory function of the brain. Cinnamon balances blood sugar levels, an important fact for people with type 2 diabetes. Cumin, another ingredient found in garam masala, fights inflammation and provides anti-oxidant properties. Cloves improve the immune system by eliminating toxins from the body.

TRIGGER HAPPY MEMORIES

My dish to relive wonderful holidays is Thai coconut curry. I experienced the silky spiciness of this dish for the first time in 1991 during a holiday in Krabi, one of the most beautiful places on the planet. Luscious green grows over towering limestone cliffs, interrupted by turquoise sea, white sand and coconut palm trees. I stayed at Phra Nang beach that you could reach only by boat. There were no motorbikes or cars. Beach shacks fed the few tourists with an amazing array of fresh seafood. I lived on coconut curry.

Nowadays you can buy Thai curry paste everywhere, but you can easily make it at home with a grinder for masalas. You can also use a mortar and pestle, but this takes longer and requires muscle. When I use ready-made curry paste, I add some fresh galangal, Thai ginger; fresh garlic and extra lemongrass. Kaffir lime leaves, fish sauce and palm sugar deepen the taste too.

There are four kinds of coconut curries: red, green, yellow and massaman (Muslim). Red is the hottest variety, made with dried red chillies and fish sauce. Green curry is made with fresh green chillies and coriander, and can be as spicy as the red paste. Yellow curry is milder and gets its colour from turmeric. Massaman curry paste is related to red curry but has spices like cinnamon, cloves and nutmeg. It is usually used for beef but also for duck and chicken.

62 THAI COCONUT CURRY

There are no fixed rules for preparing a Thai coconut curry. You can pair any kind of paste with any kind of ingredient. It all depends on your personal taste. Actually, the Thai call their coconut curry kaeng. The first Thai dictionary from 1873 AD defined kaeng as a watery broth and its ingredients do not include coconut milk. The consistency of kaeng is as individual as the choice of ingredients. If you have a curry paste, you can do Thai coconut curry.

INGREDIENTS

(Serves 4)

- 500 gm boneless chicken breasts (or any other kind of meat, fish or prawns)
- 1 carrot
- 1 red bell pepper
- 1 small zucchini
- 4 tbsp olive oil
- 3 tbsp Thai curry paste
- 2 inch piece of ginger (5 cm long)
- 4 cloves of garlic

- ❦ 2 packets coconut milk (200 ml each)
- ❦ 2 stalks lemongrass
- ❦ 2 Kaffir lime leaves (or normal lime leaves)
- ❦ Fish sauce
- ❦ Salt
- ❦ Palm sugar

METHOD

Clean protein of your choice and cut into bite-sized pieces. Clean and finely chop ginger and garlic. Heat olive oil in a big pan. Fry ginger and garlic, then add curry paste and mix well.

When oil has taken on colour of curry paste, add coconut milk. Bruise lemongrass by pressing with knife, especially the lower bit where leaves unite in a fleshy stalk. Add lemon grass and lime leaves and simmer for five minutes.

Now add vegetables and/or the protein of your choice. The sequence depends on your ingredients. Clean and cut vegetables into bite-size pieces. I slice carrot and zucchini finely at an angle and cut bell pepper into strips. Carrots and zucchini need about five minutes to cook, bell pepper only three minutes.

Chicken breasts need ten minutes. Cooking time of fish depends upon thickness. A gentle simmer for few minutes will cook most varieties. Prawns need two minutes.

When the vegetables and the proteins are cooked, season with fish sauce, salt and palm sugar. Serve immediately with steamed rice.

63 THAI CURRY PASTES

Here are the recipes for the main Thai curry pastes. They closely resemble each other. If you cannot find shrimp paste, use dried shrimps (or prawns). The method remains the same for all recipes. You can keep the curry paste for up to two weeks in a tightly sealed container in the fridge. You can also freeze it.

RED CURRY PASTE

INGREDIENTS

(Serves 8)

- 1 medium red onion, chopped
- 1 stalk fresh lemongrass, chopped
- 1 or 2 fresh red Thai chillies
- 4 cloves garlic
- 1-inch (2.5 cm) piece of galangal or ginger, sliced
- 1 tsp ground cumin
- 1 tsp ground coriander
- ½ tsp ground white (or black) pepper
- 2 tbsp fish sauce
- 1 tsp shrimp paste (or dried shrimps)
- 1 tsp sugar
- 2 tbsp ground red chillies
- 3 tbsp thick coconut milk (just enough to keep the blades turning)
- 2 tbsp lime juice

GREEN CURRY PASTE

INGREDIENTS

(Serves 8)

- 1 stalk lemongrass, minced
- 3 green chillies, sliced
- 1 small red onion
- 5 cloves garlic
- 1-inch (2.5 cm) piece of galangal or ginger, sliced
- ½ cup chopped fresh coriander leaves and stems
- ½ cup fresh basil
- 1 tsp ground cumin
- 1 tsp ground white (or black) pepper
- 1 tsp ground coriander
- 3 tbsp fish sauce
- 1 tsp shrimp paste (or dried shrimps)
- 2 tbsp lime juice
- 1 tsp brown sugar
- 3 to 4 tbsp coconut milk (enough to blend ingredients together)

YELLOW CURRY PASTE

INGREDIENTS

(Serves 8)

- 1 stalk lemongrass, chopped
- 1 or 2 yellow chillies, sliced (or 1 or 2 red chillies)
- 2 spring onions, sliced

- 🌱 1-inch (2.5 cm) piece of galangal or ginger, sliced
- 🌱 4 cloves garlic
- 🌱 1 tsp ground coriander
- 🌱 1 tsp ground cumin
- 🌱 1 tsp cumin seeds
- 🌱 ½ tsp ground cinnamon
- 🌱 2 tbsp fish sauce
- 🌱 ½ tsp shrimp paste or dried shrimps
- 🌱 2 tsp ground turmeric
- 🌱 ½ tsp ground white (or black) pepper
- 🌱 2 tbsp brown sugar
- 🌱 1 tbsp lime juice
- 🌱 3 tbsp coconut milk (enough to keep the blades moving)

MASSAMAN CURRY PASTE

INGREDIENTS

(Serves 8)

- 🌱 ¼ cup dry roasted peanuts, unsalted
- 🌱 2 shallots, sliced
- 🌱 5 cloves garlic, peeled
- 🌱 1 or 2 fresh red chillies or 1 tbsp ground red chillies
- 🌱 1-inch (2.5 cm) piece of galangal or ginger, sliced
- 🌱 1 stalk lemongrass, minced
- 🌱 1 tsp ground coriander
- 🌱 ½ tbsp ground cumin
- 🌱 1 tsp whole cumin seeds
- 🌱 ¼ tsp freshly ground nutmeg

- 🌾 1 tsp ground cinnamon
- 🌾 ½ tsp ground cloves
- 🌾 ½ tsp ground cardamom
- 🌾 2 tbsp fish sauce
- 🌾 ½ tsp shrimp paste (or dried shrimps)
- 🌾 1 tsp palm sugar or brown sugar
- 🌾 3 tbsp coconut milk (enough to keep the blades moving)

METHOD

Place all the ingredients in a food processor, chopper or blender. Process to form a paste. If the paste is too thick, add more coconut milk to help blend ingredients.

DISCOVER YOUR FAVOURITE SINS

We cannot beat about the bush; most comfort foods are dietary nightmares. But isn't it refreshing to be naughty once in a while? We are all humans and not perfect. I believe that when we dig in wholeheartedly and enjoy, we do something good.

Unfortunately, there is no recipe that fits all. Everybody's taste is different. Don't be afraid to make these recipes your own. Our bodies need all nutrients: proteins, carbohydrates and the right kinds of fat.

Who knows, maybe in a few years scientists will discover some mind-boggling news about food? Maybe there is a secret ingredient in béchamel sauce, pasta and pizza that makes it super healthy? Probably not, but there is nothing wrong with finding pleasure in food – to the contrary. The more moments of bliss we manage to enjoy, the better for all of us.

CHAPTER 6

SWEET MOMENTS OF BLISS

We all know sugar is unhealthy. There is no denying the fact. It causes caries that destroys your teeth. Sugar does not deliver any nutrients but needs B vitamins to be digested. Only the liver can break down sugar but it takes serious work. When you constantly eat a lot of sugar, you put a big strain on your liver. You also force your body to constantly produce a lot of insulin, the hormone needed to balance blood sugar levels. Over time, this leads to insulin resistance and type 2 diabetes.

Enough said … but, and this is a big but: eating sweets belongs to our culture. Although my mind told me that raising my son sugarfree would be preferable, my heart could not follow through. I could not exclude my son from birthday cakes and chocolate bars. I also believe that everything forbidden seems more attractive.

I agree with Aristotle, the ancient Greek philosopher, the man of the golden mean. When you enjoy sugar occasionally, you can steer clear of its pitfalls. Like with alcohol, we have to exercise prudence. Once in a while our body can handle sweet delights, but not on a daily basis.

I believe in fibre and complex carbohydrates as an antidote to sweet comfort food. When you indulge in sugar, you will experience a rise in blood sugar levels and then a sudden drop, leaving you with the urge to eat more sweets. You cannot avoid this but you can resist the urge.

I have experienced that I can balance my blood sugar levels by eating complex carbohydrates, delivered by whole grains, nuts and legumes, after a sugar high. Especially eating legumes works well in this case. As a rule, I only use atta, the traditional Indian whole wheat flour, for sweets.

Food alone makes nobody happy. Our bodies are complicated, awe-inspiring creations. No machine has come close to the amount of biochemical processes that make up our being. We are 'social animals'. We need family and friends and activities that further our minds, especially exercise, awareness, sunlight and sleep. Exercise does so much more than toning muscles. When you stick to a healthy lifestyle, your body can cope easily with occasional indulgences – even with sugar.

LIFESTYLE CHOICES

Many thousands of years ago we started as hunters and gatherers. We needed strong bodies that could take us places. Today, machines have overtaken a lot of the work that our ancestors had to do by hand, but our bodies were not designed to sit all day long in front of a screen.

We profit from regular exercise. It makes the heart contract more often, pumping more blood through the body. Cells receive more oxygen. The brain works better. Memory, metabolism and digestion improve. After a workout, I feel great. I religiously go to the gym thrice a week. Studies have shown that exercise boosts our mood.

Of course that does not guarantee happiness. When I feel low, I turn to rice pudding, an international classic. In the USA, rice pudding is baked and enriched with eggs, raisins and butter. In India, rice pudding is spiced with cardamom, rosewater and pistachios. As a German, I like my rice pudding with ground cinnamon and brandy-soaked raisins.

64 RICE PUDDING

For rice pudding boiled on the stovetop you need rice, milk and sugar. Unfortunately, you need to stir the pudding constantly – a rather boring task. That's why I use my pressure cooker. I prefer organic brown rice for my pudding because I like its nutty taste.

INGREDIENTS

(Serves 4)

- 1 cup brown rice
- 5 cups milk
- ½ cup sugar
- 2 tbsp ground cinnamon
- ½ tsp ground cloves

- Pinch of salt
- 1 vanilla pod or 1 tbsp vanilla essence

OPTIONAL

- ½ cup raisins soaked overnight in brandy
- ½ cup nuts of your choice
- 4 tbsp honey

> ☞ TIP: You can add any spice. This recipe does not make a very sweet pudding.

METHOD

Rinse rice and place it into a pressure cooker. Add milk, sugar, ground cinnamon, ground cloves, a pinch of salt and vanilla pod slit lengthwise. Stir well. If you want to include raisins and/or nuts, add them now.

Let it boil on low flame for thirty-five minutes after first whistle.

BROWN IS BEAUTIFUL

When you choose an ingredient, avoid the colour white whenever possible. Brown rice and whole grains offer so much more nutrition than their polished, refined versions. The process that turns brown rice into white destroys 67 per cent of the vitamin B3, 80 per cent of the vitamin B1, 90 per cent of the vitamin B6, half of the manganese, half of the phosphorus, 60 per cent of the iron, and all of the dietary fibre and essential fatty acids.

The combination of minerals, vitamins, phytonutrients and fibre in brown rice reduces the risk of colon and breast cancer, cardiovascular disease and type 2 diabetes, and lowers bad cholesterol levels.

SHAKE YOUR BOOTY

For a long time, I used to be a couch potato. I hated sports in school because I was so clumsy. The only kind of movement I liked was dancing and yoga. When I reached forty, I realised I needed to tone my muscles. Luckily I managed to get hooked by the gym.

Experts recommend we should exercise at least thirty minutes a day. You should raise your heart rate enough to sweat for five minutes. Moderate training is key. If you overdo it, harm outweighs benefits. Strenuous exercise can tear muscles and damage joints.

Without exercise, I would have gained weight during the premenopause. I have seen several friends inflate during this time. When you exercise regularly, your metabolism improves and your body burns more calories. You can indulge in sweet delights without feeling guilty.

Bread pudding is one of the timeless classics providing sweet comfort. Food historians say that it appeared in the 11th century. In England it was known as 'poor man's pudding'.

65 BREAD PUDDING

Eliza Acton describes in her cookbook *Modern Cookery*: 'Give a good flavour of lemon-rind and bitter almonds, or of cinnamon, to a pint of new milk and mix it with a quarter-pint of rich cream … Have ready in a thickly buttered dish three layers of thin bread and butter …' resulting in an utterly scrumptious bread pudding.

Basically, any kind of bread or baked goods soaked in sweetened milk and eggs, and baked in the oven deliver this pudding. You can use croissants, doughnuts or cinnamon rolls. You can add raisins, dried fruits, or whatever floats your boat. I am a girl of simple tastes and prefer vanilla and cinnamon.

I like American butterscotch sauce with my pudding. I always make a big dish. It keeps well in the fridge and tastes great when chilled.

INGREDIENTS

(Serves 8)

- 300 gm bread (1 packet toast)
- 1 litre milk
- 1 cup sugar
- 2 tbsp ground cinnamon
- 2 tbsp vanilla essence
- 4 eggs

BUTTERSCOTCH SAUCE

- 125 gm butter
- 1 cup brown sugar
- ½ cup heavy cream

METHOD

Place milk with sugar, cinnamon and vanilla into a pot over medium heat. Stir until sugar has dissolved. Let it cool down.

Cut bread into pieces. I quarter toast. Mix eggs with milk. Butter a baking dish. Place toast into baking dish, pour milk mixture over and bake at 190 degrees Celsius for thirty minutes. The mixture should set and turn golden brown.

For the butterscotch sauce, melt the butter in a saucepan. Add sugar and cream and simmer until sauce thickens.

BUTTERSCOTCH, MYSTERIOUS NAME

The flavour named butterscotch seems to have a simple name that matches its simple way of preparation. The term butterscotch was first written down in 1817 in Doncaster, a Yorkshire city. Since then it has been a popular topping for ice creams and other sweet concoctions. However, its name remains a mystery, the scotch part to be precise. Some people take it as a reference to Scotland. Others believe it comes from the word 'scorch'. Whatever the meaning, it tastes great.

BABY STEPS

If you prefer breakfast in bed to running five miles – as I do

– you might struggle with regular exercise. Start with baby steps. Find an activity that you like. Doing something for five minutes is better than doing nothing at all. Gradually increase the length. Housework is an excellent choice for exercise, leaving you with a sparkling home and a sense of achievement. I employ help but I love to clean neglected details. It gives me satisfaction (through dopamine) when I polish the faucet of the tap in my bathroom to a perfect shine.

While growing up, I always helped my mother with the housework. I peeled potatoes when my mother made potato latkes with apple sauce. Whenever she served Kartoffelpuffer (the German name) my two brothers and I competed to see who could eat the most. Usually my brothers won, but I did not lag far behind. I don't know how my mother managed to fry so many pancakes. I remember sitting in the kitchen, waiting for the pancake to arrive straight from the pan.

66 POTATO LATKES WITH APPLE SAUCE

Potato latkes don't take to sitting around. The starch in potatoes quickly turns grey. That's why you make potato latkes and eat them. Latkes are known as traditional Hanukkah food. Hanukkah dates back to 168 BC when the Syrian-Greeks seized the Jewish temple in Jerusalem and dedicated it to the worship of Zeus. When the Jews regained control, a little oil burnt for eight days, cleaning the temple. Jewish people commemorate this miracle by eating fried foods.

For a long time, housewives everywhere in potato-loving countries have produced potato pancakes. In Switzerland they are called Röstis in Austria Dotsch and in Bavaria Reiberdatschi. Potato pancakes are fried all over Eastern Europe and of course in Ireland, the country of the potato famine, where they carry the lovely name Boxty.

This is the German recipe from my childhood days. Be prepared to use a generous amount of fat for frying.

INGREDIENTS

(Makes 20)

- 2 kg potatoes
- 1 onion
- 2 big or 3 small eggs
- 2 tbsp flour
- Salt
- Oil and/or ghee for frying

APPLE SAUCE

(Makes 4 cups)

- 1 kg apples
- ½ cup water
- 3 tbsp sugar
- 1 tbsp lemon juice
- 1 tbsp ground cinnamon

METHOD

Peel and quarter apples. Cut away cores and place in a pot. Stir in lemon juice, sugar, ground cinnamon and water, and boil for fifteen minutes. Apples should be soft. Blend to smooth sauce.

Peel potatoes and onion and grate them. I use a food processor. Add eggs, flour and a pinch of salt, and mix well.

Heat oil in a big pan. Place potatoes with a big spoon in pan and spread it. Potato pancakes should be about one centimetre thick. Fry on both sides until golden brown.

Place on a plate with kitchen towels to absorb excess fat. Serve immediately with apple sauce.

APPLE SAUCE: AGE-OLD DELIGHT

The humble apple sauce is one of the oldest recipes that we still cherish today. Apple sauce remains a staple in kitchens all over the world. Its tart taste makes it compatible with sweet and savoury dishes. In medieval times apple sauce was sweetened with dates. The first recorded recipe dates back to the year 1769 and is found in Eliza Smith's cookbook *Compleat Housewife* as a condiment for duck.

WE NEED TO RELAX

Another ingredient for a happy lifestyle is meditation and rest. Many studies prove the beneficial effects of any passive relaxation technique. In the USA, people who meditate regularly show 87 per cent fewer hospitalisations for heart disease, 55 per cent fewer for tumours and 30 per cent fewer for infectious diseases. Some people claim it slows ageing, but I doubt that.

My sister-in-law has her own technique for fighting

wrinkles. 'Whenever I discover a new one, I march to the fridge and check for something yummy,' she says with a twinkle in her eyes. This method works well for the face but leads to a lot of body volume. One of her favourites is cheesecake, a classic feel-good cake.

Today, two styles of preparing cheesecake have evolved: American and German. Americans make the crust from smashed cookies mixed with butter. Germans prepare a short crust. While American bakers use cream cheese for their filling, Germans use quark, a variation of curd. The following version delivers a kind of hybrid cheesecake.

67 CREAMY CHEESECAKE

Ancient Greek moulds for cheesecakes have been discovered on the island Samos. Romans adopted this cheesecake. Since then, cheesecakes have been baked all over the world. In 1872, an American dairy farmer started to produce Philadelphia cream cheese, which led to the famous New York cheesecake.

For this cheesecake, I use hung curd and homemade paneer together with cream. I have used orange liqueur to flavour the crust and the filling. It is important to stir the cheese mixture carefully. You don't want to incorporate a lot of air.

INGREDIENTS

(For a springform of 24 cm/9.5 in)

🍴 125 gm butter

- ¼ cup sugar
- 1½ cups flour
- 2 tbsp orange liqueur (or zest of 1 lemon)
- 4 tbsp cold water
- Butter to grease the springform

FILLING

- 2 cups hung curd
- 2 cups paneer
- 200 ml cream
- 3 eggs
- 1 cup sugar
- ½ cup rum raisins
- 2 tbsp orange liqueur
- 1 tbsp vanilla essence

METHOD

Cut butter into cubes. Place flour in a bowl. Add orange liqueur, sugar and water and mix lightly with a spoon. Rub butter into flour and work it gently. When mixture resembles sticky crumbles, wrap in cling film. Rest in the fridge for thirty minutes. Butter springform.

For filling prepare curd and paneer as described in chapter 'Kitchen Must-Haves'. Place curd in a bowl. Grate paneer. Add with cream, sugar, eggs, rum raisins, orange liqueur and vanilla essence. Stir gently.

Roll out dough between two sheets of cling film to cover bottom of springform. Use rest of dough to cover sides. Place a pot with hot water at bottom of oven. Steam will help to bake cheesecake. Cook for at least one and a half hours at 150 degrees Celsius. Filling should have set and wiggle only a bit. Cool down slowly in oven.

DRIED OR FRESH FRUIT?

When you try to understand if dried fruit like raisins are healthy, you can land in a pickle. While some people praise dried fruit, others warn about additives and the loss of vitamins during drying. One thing seems clear: when fruit is dried, many of the water soluble vitamins including vitamin C and B, and potassium are lost. But there remain substantial amounts of minerals like calcium and iron, fibre and plenty of antioxidants in the dried fruits, making them a valuable addition to our diet. Experts name dried prunes, raisins and figs as the healthiest dried fruits. However, sulphur used to preserve dried fruit can cause stomach and bowel irritation in sensitive people.

OVERCOMING BINGE EATING

Meditation helped me overcome my eating disorders. During my first marriage, I had thought that my food addiction was a thing of the past. I could not have been more wrong. The moment I decided to divorce, binge eating returned with a vengeance, like a well-known nightmare. In a few months I piled on several kilograms.

Again, I could not control my hands stuffing food into my mouth. But this time, I did not suffer in silence. I went to my doctor. He immediately prescribed psychotherapy. Thanks to the social system in Germany, my health insurance paid the considerable cost.

It is impossible to describe what happened in therapy. My therapist, a woman, used trance journeys and talk therapy. In the course of one year she made me realize how wounds from my childhood still affected me.

I read everything I could find about eating disorders. My favourite book – still relevant – is *Fat Is a Feminist Issue* by Susie Orbach. The German title *Anti-Diet Book* fits better, I think. It deals with the way women perceive and use their bodies. If you fight with eating disorders, try to read it. This book was an eye-opener for me.

During a holiday I visited McLeodganj in Himachal Pradesh. I was just looking at some Thangkas, Tibetan paintings depicting Buddhist deities, when a young man approached me. 'I am starting a meditation workshop tomorrow. Please do come,' he said.

I showed up at the meeting place, a round courtyard paved with flagstones, just a few metres from the spring in Baghsu Nag. He taught the Shambhala method, a technique of working with the breath. This teacher motivated me so much that I managed to meditate two times a day for half an hour for many years.

Travelling has shaped my personality as much as my Catholic Bavarian upbringing. Some years ago, we visited the Florida Keys, a chain of islands that divides the Gulf of Mexico from the Atlantic Ocean. Until 1930, people in the Keys had to make do without fresh milk because there was not enough green for domestic animals to eat. Then the Overseas

Highway was built and trucks could reach the islands from the mainland. The ocean is clean, clear and turquoise. The people are friendly, and happy hour starts at 4 p.m.

Since then, I wanted to bake key lime pie, the signature dish of the islands. I finally did it when a friend gave me some limes from a tree in her garden. This tree grows in a beautiful place in Goa. Waves break on the rocks that surround this peaceful garden on two sides. Peacocks populate the hillock overlooking it.

68 KEY LIME PIE

My friend has grown up in the States and knows a lot about its cuisine. When I have a question concerning food, she is one of the people I turn to. When I mentioned key lime pie, she suggested to make the crust with cookies, and to never, ever use fresh milk to make the filling. I decided to top it with Italian meringue.

There are three different kinds of meringue: French, Swiss and Italian. For French meringue, one drizzles sugar into the egg whites while beating them. Stirring together egg whites and sugar in a double boiler and then whipping the hot mixture makes Swiss meringue. Italian meringue is done with hot sugar syrup beaten into egg whites.

INGREDIENTS

(For a 24 cm/9.5 in pie dish)

- 175 gm Graham or digestive biscuits
- 80 gm butter

- 🍐 2 tbsp sugar
- 🍐 ½ tbsp lime zest
- 🍐 Butter for the pie dish

FILLING

- 🍐 1 can sweetened condensed milk (400 gm)
- 🍐 2 tbsp lime zest
- 🍐 ½ cup lime juice
- 🍐 4 egg yolks

MERINGUE

- 🍐 4 egg whites
- 🍐 1 tbsp lime juice
- 🍐 2 tbsp icing sugar
- 🍐 1¼ cup sugar
- 🍐 ½ cup water

METHOD

Preheat oven to 180 degrees Celsius. Crumble biscuits in a blender and place in a bowl. Melt butter; add sugar, lime zest and butter to bowl and mix well. Grate lime zest with a micro plane. Avoid white, bitter layer under lime skin. Butter pie dish and cover bottom and sides with crust. Bake for ten minutes.

Pour condensed milk in a bowl. Add lime zest and lime juice, and stir. Separate eggs. Place egg whites into a bowl and add egg yolks to condensed milk. Mix and pour over crust. Bake for another ten minutes.

Place water and sugar into a pot over medium flame. Stir until sugar has dissolved. Boil to softball stage: a bit of syrup dropped in a glass of cold water remains a ball that you can shape.

Beat egg whites. Gradually add lime juice and icing sugar. Beat until soft peaks form, and then pour in sugar syrup slowly while beating. The meringue should develop a glossy shine.

Spread it over hot pie and bake for fifteen minutes. The meringue should turn golden brown. You cannot keep this pie longer than one day.

LIMES: FULL OF VITAMIN C

The scent of fresh limes or lemons lifts our spirits like little else. They provide a bounty of vitamin C, which can be easily absorbed as it is coupled with the B vitamins niacin and thiamine. These citrus fruits have more potassium than apples or grapes, which is favourable to the heart. Lime juice destroys the bacteria of cholera, diphtheria, typhoid and other deadly diseases. Although lemon juice is so full of acid we cannot take it in its pure form, it actually leaves alkaline residues in the body. It cures many digestion problems like heartburn, nausea, biliousness and constipation. It even eases hiccups.

Lemon juice taken regularly in the morning stimulates the liver and dissolves gallstones. It also alleviates symptoms of asthma, tonsillitis and sore throat, and helps with urinary tract infections and high uric acid problems such as arthritis or rheumatism.

VOICES IN MY HEAD

You can call meditation training of the mind. When you sit for half an hour watching your breath, you cannot escape your inner dialogue. Thoughts carry you away and you have to return to your breath. Over time, you create distance with your chattering mind. Thanks to this distance, I realized there are different voices in my head.

And I noticed how unfriendly these voices behaved. My psychotherapist helped me identify the voices. One voice – I called it the master of torture – constantly put me down. As soon as I relaxed, it called me lazy. For every mistake, I had to endure abuse. I finally understood the enormous pressure inside my mind. Stuffing myself with food was a way to relieve the tension.

Thanks to meditation, I changed these voices and I could live in the here and now. Doing meditation on your own requires a lot of discipline. Fortunately, there are many apps in the market with all kinds of guided meditations, relaxation exercises and binaural sounds. Many of them are free. Lie down comfortably in your bed and listen to them.

I hear guided meditations after the gym. Sometimes I also use the magic window for eating sweets after a workout. With my belly blissfully digesting cinnamon rolls – or some other sweet – I visualize calm vibrations. Cinnamon rolls have a special place in my heart; they can be found in unlikely places. When I visited Nepal for the first time in 1986, we splurged some of our money on a breakfast at the Pumpernickel Bakery in Kathmandu. On offer – next to croissants, cheesecake and chocolate brownies – were cinnamon rolls.

After the Himalayas, we travelled to Goa, which was a wild place then.

Goa was famous in those days for beach parties. They started in the middle of the night and lasted until sunrise. In the morning, local bakers delivered coconut cake, croissants and cinnamon rolls.

69 DELICIOUS SPIRALS

My cinnamon rolls always sport some kind of nuts. They add taste and texture. Coconut flakes are affordable and oh-so-yummy – when they mingle with cinnamon, sugar and butter.

INGREDIENTS

(Makes 20)

- 4½ cups flour
- ½ cup cornstarch
- 2 packets dry yeast
- ½ cup sugar
- Salt
- ¾ cup milk
- 100 gm butter

FILLING

- 1½ cups sugar
- 3 tbsp cinnamon powder
- 100 gm butter

🌱 1 cup desiccated coconut flakes
🌱 Butter for cookie sheet

ICING

🌱 2 cups icing sugar

☞ **TIP**: You can use any kind of nuts. You can also omit them.

METHOD

Place two tablespoons sugar in a small bowl, add a quarter cup of water and dry yeast and stir well.

Put milk and butter into a pot and melt butter. Let it cool down. Place flour, cornstarch and sugar into a bowl. Make a hole in middle and pour yeast mixture inside. Cover with flour. When cracks appear, add milk and a pinch of salt. Knead to smooth dough. Let it rise until it has doubled in volume, about one hour. Knead again. Roll it to a rectangular shape on a floured surface. Spread soft butter over dough; sprinkle evenly with sugar, cinnamon and coconut flakes. Roll up dough as tightly as you can.

Cut roll into slices about two centimetres thick using dental floss. Slide it under roll into position, cross over roll and pull. Place rolls onto a buttered cookie sheet and let rise for another hour. Bake at 180 degrees Celsius for thirty-five to forty minutes.

Mix icing sugar with a little water to a thick cream and brush over cinnamon rolls.

GOOD AND BAD KINDS OF YEAST

Many people automatically think 'infection' when they hear the word 'yeast'. Candida albicans is the kind of yeast we all should try to avoid. This fungus is normally found on our skin. It can grow out of control and cause itchy infections when our immune system is weakened, for example, after a course of antibiotics. However, food grade yeast packs quite a few goodies for our bodies. This fungus converts sugars and starches via fermentation into carbon dioxide and alcohol and thus makes bread and sweet dough rise nicely. At the same time it delivers a healthy amount of B vitamins, minerals and proteins.

TEST OF TIME

Many sweets date back a long time, including the following recipe, profiteroles.

The beginnings of this sweet reach far back. Legend has it that the chef of Catherine de Medici named Panterelli invented the choux pastry in 1540. Over time this dough was used to make cakes stuffed with sweet and savoury fillings. The father of classical French cuisine, Marie-Antoine Carême, immortalized the choux pastry by describing it in his cookbook *Pâtissier Royal*.

Profiteroles have to be fresh because they turn damp quickly. Soggy profiteroles disappoint. You need the delightful contrast of crunch, sweet softness and almost bitter chocolate.

70 PROFITEROLES

Baking profiteroles requires technique and a lot can go wrong. The most difficult task is to gauge how many eggs to incorporate into the choux pastry. Not enough or too much will prevent the dough from rising. Bake them long enough. They need to turn golden brown all around, otherwise they deflate. My profiteroles need at least one hour in the oven.

INGREDIENTS

(Makes 24)

- 1½ cups whole wheat flour
- 1½ cups (300 ml) water
- 125 gm butter
- 3 tbsp sugar
- 1 pinch salt
- 3 or 4 eggs

CRÈME PÂTISSIÈRE

- 500 ml milk
- 30 gm butter
- 1 cup castor sugar
- 4 egg yolks
- ¼ cup corn flour
- ¼ cup whole wheat flour
- 1 vanilla pod

TOPPING

🍷 100 gm dark chocolate
🍷 50 ml espresso coffee or Nescafé

METHOD

Preheat oven to 200 degrees Celsius. Place water, butter, sugar and salt in a pot and bring to a boil. Stir well. Add flour in one go and stir. Keep stirring until dough forms into a ball and coats bottom of pot. Keep stirring over medium heat for three more minutes. Let it cool down and add eggs one by one. The dough has to develop a glossy shine but needs to remain firm and hold its shape after piping.

Pipe balls onto a buttered cookie sheet. Smooth surface with a knife dipped into water. Place profiteroles into hot oven and don't open it for at least half an hour. Then turn profiteroles upside down. They need to turn golden brown all over. I have baked profiteroles for one and a half hours for optimum results.

For crème, place milk and butter in a pot. Slice open vanilla pod, scrape out seeds and add to milk with half of sugar. Bring to a gentle boil while stirring. When milk has bubbled, switch off heat and let infuse for fifteen minutes.

Place egg yolks in a bowl. Beat with a hand mixer and add remaining sugar gradually to avoid curdling.

Mix corn and whole wheat flour with egg mix while stirring continuously. Add one third of milk to egg cream. Bring milk to a boil and add egg mix. At this point it should set immediately once it burps. Let it cool down, covered with cling film.

When crème and puffs have cooled, fill crème into a piping bag with a thin nozzle. Push nozzle into puffs and fill them. Melt chocolate with coffee in a double boiler and cover profiteroles.

☞ **TIP:** Some people prefer profiteroles with ice cream: halve the profiteroles and place a scoop of ice cream in the middle.

CARÊME, THE FIRST CELEBRITY CHEF

Marie-Antoine Carême (1783–1833), the father of classical French cuisine, dedicated his life to gastronomic pleasure and wrote abundantly. He proves that anyone can gain immortal fame. His parents abandoned him in Paris at the height of the French Revolution. He started to work as a kitchen boy and became the apprentice of a famous pâtissier. Carême opened a pastry shop where he displayed elaborate cake constructions, sometimes modelled after historic monuments. He also worked for the French diplomat Charles Maurice de Talleyrand-Périgord.

Talleyrand – and indirectly Carême – became famous during the Congress of Vienna that followed the fall of Napoléon and altered the culinary taste of the upper classes of Europe. Carême invented the toque, the chef's hat, and classified sauces into four groups. He wrote numerous cookbooks, above all the encyclopaedic *L'Art de la Cuisine Française*. Carême died young at forty-nine, possibly because he spent years in the toxic fumes of charcoal ovens used for cooking then.

LET THE SUNSHINE IN

Another essential ingredient is sunlight. I grew up in Bavaria where winter never seems to end. During holidays, I craved for sun. Doctors coined the term 'Seasonal Affective Disorder' (SAD) to describe depression caused by lacking light. SAD is common in countries with long winters.

Living in Goa, I don't crave for sun any more. I usually take a sunbath after a workout in the gym, drinking coconut water. As a child, I had no idea that you could drink water from coconuts. I only knew desiccated coconut flakes from the following recipe.

71 COCONUT TRIANGLES

As a child I could not get enough of my mother's coconut triangles. Sweet, crunchy coconut combined with apricot jam and chocolate makes me happy – and my guests too.

INGREDIENTS

(Makes 24)

- 2 cups flour
- 1 tsp baking powder
- 3 cups sugar
- 2 tbsp vanilla essence
- 2 eggs

- 🍶 400 gm butter
- 🍶 400 gm desiccated coconut flakes
- 🍶 300 gm apricot jam
- 🍶 300 gm dark chocolate

METHOD

Put flour in a bowl. Add baking powder, one cup sugar, one tablespoon vanilla essence, eggs and 150 grams butter cut into cubes. Knead to smooth dough.

Spread butter over cookie sheet. Roll out dough between two sheets of cling film to cover cookie sheet. Spread apricot jam over dough.

Place 200 grams of butter in a pot. Add two cups sugar, one tablespoon vanilla essence, desiccated coconut and four tablespoons water. Bring to a boil over low heat while stirring. If it is very thick, add a bit more water.

Let cool down and spread over apricot jam. Bake for thirty to forty minutes at 200 degrees Celsius. The coconut should turn golden-brown. Let it cool down for ten minutes.

Cut into twelve rectangles, and then slice every rectangle into two triangles. Melt cooking chocolate with remaining butter in a double boiler. Stir well, and spread over corners of triangles. Keep on a rack until chocolate has set.

AMAZING MONKEY FACE

Spanish explorers named the beautiful coconut palm tree 'coco', or monkey face, because the three 'eyes' at the base of the coconut resemble a face. In Sanskrit it is called 'kalpavriksha', which means 'tree which gives all that is necessary for living'. The trunk is wood; leaves can be woven into mats. The husk can be made into fibre called coir, used for brushes, mats, fishnets and rope.

An average coconut tree yields sixty coconuts per year. Coconut water is a natural isotonic drink with the same electrolytic composition as our blood. The health benefits of coconut products include stress relief, boosting good cholesterol levels, increased immunity, proper digestion and metabolism, relief from kidney problems and heart disease. Coconuts contain a wealth of minerals and vitamins. Although coconut's fatty acids are saturated, they belong to the kind our bodies need and absorb easily. Some people even swear that coconut fat is slimming.

REALITY CHECK

Fear of skin cancer keeps many people away from sunlight or makes them use toxic sunscreen lotions. I think we need a reality check. Exposure to sunlight makes us feel good. Sunlight helps our body produce vitamin D, improves Alzheimer's disease and skin disorders like psoriasis, acne, eczema and fungal infections. It increases the oxygen content of human blood and the production of white blood cells.

Twenty minutes of sunlight a day hurt nobody and do a lot of good. How long you should stay in the sun depends on the time of day, where you live and the colour of the skin. Fair skin absorbs ultraviolet rays faster than darker skin. Some experts recommend limiting your stay in the sun to strictly twenty minutes. I don't believe in living by rules. However, I try not to stay longer than half an hour or so in the sun.

I am happy when I can soak up sun three times a week. Running a house and keeping a family fed is a lot of work, but I would not have it any other way. It makes me happy when I know I dish up something nice like the following sweet.

Few recipe names spread the feeling of home and hearth like the words 'apple crumble'. I have enriched the crumble with coconut flakes and oats. Actually, this turns my crumble into a crisp. The difference between a cobbler, a crumble and a crisp lies in the flour. All use fruits baked in the oven. Cobblers are prepared with biscuit dough like the French classic Clafoutis. Crumbs are topped with a mixture of flour, sugar and butter, while crisps include oats and nuts in the topping.

72 APPLE CRUMBLE

Some people call apple crumble the quintessential British pudding. I know apple crumble pie as a typical German dish. We know from colonial times that British do tend to appropriate countries and culinary achievements. They also tend to know everything.

INGREDIENTS

(Serves 6)

- 1 kg apples
- ¼ cup sugar
- 2 tbsp cinnamon powder
- 1 tsp ground cloves
- 2 tbsp lemon juice

- 2 tbsp flour
- ½ cup rum raisins
- Butter for the baking dish

CRUMBLE

- 1 cup desiccated coconut flakes
- 1 cup flour
- 1½ cups rolled oats
- ¾ cup brown sugar
- 150 gm butter
- ½ tbsp cinnamon powder
- ½ tsp ground cloves

METHOD

Butter a baking dish. I use a pie form with a diameter of twenty-seven centimetres (eleven inches).

Peel and quarter apples; cut away core. Halve each apple quarter. Boil for ten minutes with one tablespoon lemon juice and two tablespoons sugar. Place apples in a mixing bowl; add sugar, cinnamon, clove powder, lemon juice, rum raisins and flour. Combine well and fill into the baking dish.

For crumble, place flour, oats, sugar, ground cinnamon and cloves into a bowl. Combine well. Cut butter into cubes and rub into dry mix.

Spread crumbles over apples and bake at 190 degrees Celsius for forty to fifty minutes until crumble turns golden brown.

☞ TIP: You can use any kind of nuts in the crumble or substitute them with the same amount of flour.

BRITISH INVENTION?

British cooks want to make us believe that apple crumble was invented in Britain during the Second World War (WW II). British housewives omitted the piecrust to save on flour, sugar and fat, and apple crumble was born.

However, apple crisps or crumbles have been around for quite some time before WW II. In the 19th century, apple crumble pie was one of the most common home-baked cakes in Northern Germany. Isabel Ely Lord has mentioned an apple crisp in *Everybody's Cookbook: A Comprehensive Manual of Home Cookery*, published in 1924 in New York. Recipes have crossed borders as long as human beings have wandered around. If the British want to appropriate the apple crumble, let them have it.

POISONOUS LOTIONS

Doctors and scientists keep telling us to apply sunscreen lotion. A test showed that nine of the fifteen allowed chemical sunscreens in the USA are endocrine disruptors; they disturb the function of hormones and can do a lot of damage. Creams diffuse through the skin and enter the blood stream. I used tons of sunscreen lotions when I was young. Occasionally, I still use sun protection when I know I will be exposed for a long time. In general, I make do without them.

Maybe I would use more sunscreen if I could make sense of ingredients for cosmetics, but I have enough to do with keeping informed about food ingredients. For example, some years ago I discovered that gelatine is made from bones, rendering normal panna cotta unfit for vegetarians. This dish rides the wave of zeitgeist. Fans declared it the ultimate Italian spoon dessert.

73 VEGETARIAN PANNA COTTA

Egg whites bind this panna cotta perfectly. You get a wonderfully creamy dessert that is made in five minutes (if you don't consider the baking time). Because panna cotta is rich and creamy, I serve it with fruits.

INGREDIENTS

(For 4 ramekins of 175 ml)

- 1½ cups cream (300 ml)
- 1 cup milk (200 ml)
- ¾ cup icing sugar
- 3 egg whites
- 2 tbsp homemade vanilla essence

STRAWBERRY SAUCE

- 500 gm strawberries or cherries
- 3 tbsp icing sugar
- 3 tbsp port wine

METHOD

Heat two litres of water in a pot.

If you use vanilla bean instead of essence, slice it open and simmer for one minute in milk. Mix icing sugar with vanilla essence and milk. Add cream and egg whites and stir gently. Be careful not to impart air.

Fill mixture into ramekins. Spread a kitchen towel over bottom of a deep baking dish. Place ramekins into dish and fill it with almost boiling water.

Bake in the oven for sixty minutes at 160 degrees Celsius. Let cool down in water bath, then refrigerate for two hours. If you want to unmould it, slide a knife around ramekin and turn it upside down onto a plate.

Clean and halve strawberries or cherries. Macerate with sugar and port wine for half an hour, then puree half of fruit. Mix it with macerated fruit and serve with panna cotta.

ORIGIN OF GELATINE

I was always disturbed by the use of gelatine in this recipe. Panna cotta means, literally translated, cooked cream. This dish comes from Piedmont, a region in Northern Italy around Torino, the capital of Italian kings. The original recipe had fish bones simmered together with cream. Actually, gelatine is still called colla di pesce (glue of fish) in Italy.

RED-HOT FIRE SHOVEL

The application of heat can result in disaster or delight, and the line between the two can be quite thin. The correct amount of heat is vital for the following recipe: crème brûlée, the French version of panna cotta. However, this pudding has first been served in the mid-1600s at Trinity College in Cambridge. These early intellectuals must have been well-fed, indeed.

In 1691, the French chef François Massialot published the recipe for crème brûlée in his cookbook *Le Cuisinier Royal et Bourgeoise*. Later he renamed it crème anglaise, English cream. He used a red-hot fire shovel to burn the sugar on top of the cream into caramel. Today, a blowtorch is used. Unfortunately, I don't own a blowtorch so I looked for ways to prepare this dessert without one.

74 CRÈME BRÛLÉE

Melting sugar to caramel is a delicate process and burns in seconds. I prefer making dry caramel in a pan and pouring it over the cream. However, some of my guests complained that the caramel was too thick.

That's why I tried another technique, resembling the original method: I took a round ladle that fitted the top of my ramekins, heated it up in the fire of the gas stove and pressed it gently onto a thin layer of sugar granules. This does not result in such an even layer but works quite well. You get a layer so thin that it even found my friends' approval.

INGREDIENTS

(For 4 ramekins of 175 ml)

🍮 400 ml cream

- ❦ 4 egg yolks
- ❦ 1/3 cup sugar
- ❦ 1 tbsp homemade vanilla essence or 1 vanilla bean or ½ tbsp commercial vanilla essence

CARAMEL

- ❦ ½ cup sugar

METHOD

This recipe relies on vanilla flavour. Place cream in a pot. If you use a vanilla bean, slit it open, scrape out seeds and mix bean and seeds with cream – or combine vanilla essence with cream. Add sugar and bring to a boil over medium heat. Stir frequently.

When the cream has come to a boil, let it cool down for 5 minutes. Place egg yolks in a bowl. Strain cream and pour into egg yolks while stirring continuously. Fill mixture into ramekins.

Spread a kitchen towel over bottom of a deep baking dish. Put ramekins into the dish and fill it up with hot water. Bake for forty-five minutes at 160 degrees Celsius. Let cool down in oven, then refrigerate.

Finish crème brûlée shortly before serving. Melt sugar over medium heat in a pan with a heavy bottom to dry caramel (check recipe for dry caramel) and pour it quickly over cream. Or sprinkle a thin layer of sugar on top of cold cream. Take a ladle that fits your ramekins and hold it into gas fire. Place it gently on top of sugar layer to make caramel. You can repeat if sugar has not caramelized evenly.

ROSES IN DISGUISE

Apricots make me happy. My uncle had a big apricot tree in his garden. His wife, my aunt, turned most apricots into stew. She simply cooked the apricots with white wine until they fell apart. It was served with liquid, fresh cream and sugar. You also find apricots in India.

'Amazingly, almost all the fruits grown in home gardens, from strawberries to apricots, are members of the same plant family, Rosaceae, along with such decorative favourites as roses, mountain ash and quince,' states garden expert Diane E. Bilderbeck. This explains why you find similar fruits all over the world. Apricots are the star of the following, traditional Indian recipe.

75 QUBANI KA MEETHA

Hyderabadi cuisine is famous for its dum biryani but also for qubani ka meetha. Every wedding in Hyderabad features this dessert.

Qubani ka meetha is similar to the stew of my childhood, made from dried apricots. Dried apricots remind me of Likir, a Buddhist monastery in Ladakh that I visited during my trip with the Enfield. The window front of its guest room offers a splendid view over a valley with apricot trees. While meditating, I saw the trees swaying in the summer breeze.

This sweet is easy to prepare, a great dessert for dinner parties. Indians serve it with ice cream, fresh cream or custard. It goes well with panna cotta also.

INGREDIENTS

(Serves 4)

- 🍴 200 gm dried apricots
- 🍴 ½ cup sugar (optional)
- 🍴 1 cinnamon quill or 1 tbsp ground cinnamon or 1 tbsp ground cardamom
- 🍴 1 tbsp lemon or lime juice (optional)
- 🍴 1 tsp saffron strands (optional)

METHOD

Place apricots in a bowl, cover with water and soak overnight. Halve and deseed them and place with soaking water in a pot.

Bring to a boil and simmer until they fall apart. Add sugar, saffron and lime juice fifteen minutes into the cooking, if needed. Crack open seeds and gather nuts.

Qubani ka meetha is ready when the cooking water has reduced to a thick syrup. Combine with nuts and serve.

SUPPORT FOR BLOOD PRESSURE

Apricots originated in central Asia around 3000 BC; along the Silk Road it reached the Middle East. Apricots were known in ancient Greece and the Roman Empire. Drying fruits destroys some vitamins but concentrates minerals. Dried apricots are an excellent source for potassium. Lack of potassium can lead to high blood pressure. They also contain a lot of iron and plenty of beta-carotene that can be converted to vitamin A, an antioxidant that supports the immune system, cell growth and vision.

GIVE YOURSELF SOME SUGAR

There is no way we can sweet-talk sugar. It would be best for all of us to avoid this substance completely. Sugar substitutes don't offer a solution because they are at least as harmful as the real thing. Still, to say it with Mary Poppins, 'a spoonful of sugar makes the medicine go down'. A bit of sweetness can brighten your day and help you overcome low moments. When you lead a healthy lifestyle, you can indulge occasionally. What would life be without it?

CHAPTER 7

THE CHOCOLATE HEAVEN

Chocolate can be a shortcut to heaven. Savouring chocolate – or any other delicacy – can turn into a meditative experience. When you concentrate on tasting food, you have to be in the moment, free from thinking. Because chocolate melts slowly, it is perfect for practising awareness. Savour the rich, pampering sensations chocolates offer.

Chocolate does not make you fat, only over-indulging does. Studies have shown that the first bite of everything tastes the best. The next few bites are still rewarding. Then our taste buds grow tired and we might as well stop eating. At this point gluttony sets in and most of us finish our delicious plate.

I strongly believe in the healing power of chocolate. Before it reaches your mouth, chocolate has undertaken a long journey starting at the tree 'Theobroma Cacao'. Theobroma means 'food for gods', literally translated from ancient Greek. This native plant of central America is now grown everywhere in the tropics.

Some years ago scientists discovered that chocolate is healthy. It delivers amazing amounts of minerals and antioxidants. It improves blood flow, lowers blood pressure and protects from cardiac diseases. It also improves how your brain works. However, not every chocolate is healthy. You need a serious amount of cacao to feel a difference. Readymade chocolate bars don't count, only dark chocolate with a high amount of cocoa. I recommend home-cooked or baked goods with prime ingredients.

Unfortunately, it can be difficult to find really good chocolate. For years, I used cooking chocolate because imported chocolate was too expensive. Cooking chocolate is usually made with hydrogenated vegetable oils. That means, oils are mixed with hydrogen to make them more solid, resulting in trans fat, the horrible kind of fat that clogs the arteries. There is little or no cacao butter involved. Good quality chocolate only contains cacao butter, no other fat. If you can, use Swiss, Italian or German chocolate. I don't trust American varieties because they have a lot of chemical additives.

Luckily, in recent years, leading Indian chocolate producers have started to make high quality chocolate with cacao butter. These products have changed the Indian market completely. Now good quality chocolate, made in India, is available. India is using around 30,000 tons of cacao seeds a year and the production keeps increasing. Because of the high demand, farmers in south India have started to grow cacao.

This new Indian chocolate is significantly more expensive than cooking chocolate but only one third of the price of imported chocolate. I keep using it for all my chocolate recipes.

HOLE IN THE HEART

Some experts believe that educating binge eaters to chew with awareness stops them from gorging. Education might work with careless eaters. If you suffer from an eating disorder, training is useless and logic does not apply. Addiction to food will always overpower your rational mind. But it helps to remember that awareness multiplies the pleasure of food, especially chocolate.

Baking and cooking with chocolate has a long tradition in most countries. In the German speaking part of Europe it was mostly used for cakes. No other chocolate cake has been fought over and written about as much as the Sachertorte – invented in Vienna, the capital of the Austrian Empire. Its history starts in 1832 in the house of Fürst Metternich who hosted the Congress of Vienna in 1815. This year-long event decided the destiny of Europe after the reign of Napoléon Bonaparte.

During the Congress, Metternich kept the visiting monarchs in a jolly mood by all possible means, especially good food. Historians believe that Metternich's diplomacy changed the culinary taste of Europe's upper classes.

CREATED BY AN APPRENTICE

Fürst Metternich also inspired the Sachertorte, albeit many years after the Congress of Vienna. He asked his kitchen to prepare a special dessert for important guests, not knowing that his pastry chef had fallen ill. The sixteen-year-old apprentice Franz Sacher stepped up to the plate and created the cake.

His son Eduard later made his father's cake famous while working for the Café Demel in Vienna. In 1876, Eduard opened a luxury hotel that went bankrupt. In 1938, the new owners of the hotel started to sell 'The Original Sachertorte'. A fierce legal battle broke out that lasted until 1963, when the parties settled out of court. The Hotel Sacher is now allowed to sell The Original Sachertorte, while the Café Demel sells the 'Eduard Sachertorte'. The so-called original has a layer of apricot jam in the middle, while the Eduard one only sports jam under the chocolate cover.

76 SACHERTORTE

My recipe comes to you from my mother who uses jam only under the chocolate cover.

INGREDIENTS

(For a 24 cm/9.5 in springform)

- 150 gm dark chocolate
- 150 gm butter
- ½ cup sugar
- ¼ cup icing sugar
- 6 eggs
- 1¼ cups flour
- 1 tsp baking powder

ICING

- 🍴 Apricot jam
- 🍴 200 gm dark chocolate
- 🍴 30 gm butter

> ☞ **TIP:** You can add three tablespoons espresso coffee or coffee liqueur to the icing. You can also halve the cake and put extra jam in the middle.

METHOD

Prepare springform by lining the bottom with baking paper. Sachertorte is a biscuit cake. That means eggs are separated and then folded back together. You never grease a baking dish for biscuit cakes because it would hinder rising.

Break chocolate into pieces and melt with butter in a double boiler, a small pot inside a bigger one filled with hot water. Never melt chocolate over direct flame.

Stir together and let it cool down. Place in a bowl, add sugar and combine. Separate eggs. Whisk egg yolks into chocolate mixture.

Beat egg whites to soft peaks. I always use an electric hand mixer. Sift icing sugar over egg whites and beat to stiff peaks.

Slide egg whites onto chocolate mixture. Mix flour with baking powder and sift over egg whites. Carefully fold everything together.

Bake at 190 degrees Celsius for forty to fifty minutes. A toothpick inserted in middle should come out clean. Let cake cool down, slide a knife around sides and turn it onto a plate. Warm up apricot jam and spread over top and sides of cake. Melt chocolate and butter for icing and cover cake.

SUGAR – INDIAN INVENTION

Crystallized sugar was developed in India around the 5th century, during the reign of the Imperial Guptas. In 1498, Portuguese navigator Vasco da Gama brought sugar from India to Lisbon that became the European sugar capital. By the 1800s, sugar was widely available to upper and middle classes in Europe.

Nowadays, sugar is produced all over the world from two plants: sugar beets and sugarcane. To produce raw sugar, the juice of sugarcane or beets is mixed with lime. A drying process produces granules.

To obtain white sugar, phosphoric acid and calcium hydroxide are added to sugar cane juice before further processing.

Commercial brown sugar is refined white sugar mixed with molasses syrup, then dried again, making it the worst sugar, considering the impact on the environment. It requires all the processes of refined white sugar plus additional mixing and drying.

THE DARK SIDE OF CACAO

All his life, my husband has eaten what he wanted and never had to struggle with his weight. Our son is growing and his appetite is as enormous as his length. Both my men are serious chocoholics and can demolish astonishing amounts.

Most likely the cacao in your chocolate has grown in Africa. 70 per cent of the world's cacao comes from Africa. To make chocolate, cacao powder is mixed with sugar and run through steel rollers to achieve a fine texture. A chocolate-making machine conches this mix into what we know as chocolate. This machine mixes the powder with the cacao butter and aerates the chocolate, giving it its texture. This process can last from a few hours until six days for expensive quality. Finally, chocolate is tempered several times to give it a fine, glossy look.

Unfortunately, the chocolate industry has a very dark side. Experts estimate that 40 per cent of all cacao is grown with slave work, especially child slaves. They work under terrible conditions. You can avoid supporting slave labour by buying only chocolate from fair trade organisations, organic chocolate or imported chocolate. The German company Ritter Sport and the Swiss company Lindt have pledged to use only properly sourced cacao. Nestlé, Hershey's and Ferrero have promised to avoid cacao made with slave labour by 2020, a rather generous goal for these massive companies, if you ask me.

77 BROWNIES

When I announce chocolate brownies I can count on happy smiles. You can prepare a big amount with relatively little effort. Needless to say, I take the biggest baking dish I have. Never, ever have any of my brownies survived for longer than two days.

INGREDIENTS

(Makes 30)

- 500 gm dark chocolate
- 280 gm butter
- 5 eggs
- 2 cups sugar
- 2 cups flour
- 1 tbsp vanilla essence
- 3 tbsp coffee
- ¼ cup cacao powder
- 2 teaspoons baking powder
- 200 gm walnuts
- Butter to grease the baking dish (35x25 cm or 14x10 in)

METHOD

Cover bottom and sides of baking dish with butter. Melt 250 grams chocolate with 200 grams butter in a double boiler. When water is boiling switch off the flame and wait until chocolate has melted. Be careful: overheating ruins chocolate. Combine mixture well.

Chop walnuts roughly. Preheat oven to 180 degrees Celsius. Crack eggs into a mixing bowl, add sugar and vanilla essence and beat with a hand-mixer to a thick cream. Blend baking powder with flour; sieve over egg mixture and combine.

Fold in chocolate mixture and walnuts. Fill dough into dish and bake at 190 degrees Celsius for around thirty minutes, until mixture has just set.

Let cool down in dish, then turn onto a wire rack. Melt remaining 250 grams chocolate in a double boiler with remaining butter. Mix well and cover brownies. Let it set before cutting into pieces.

☞ **TIP:** Always melt chocolate in a double boiler! For a double boiler you need two pots, one fitting into the other. Place the chocolate into the small pot. Fill water into the big pot, place the small into the big pot and put it on the fire. You can also melt chocolate in the microwave at medium. Start with one minute and then at intervals of thirty seconds.

AMAZING PROPERTIES

The Olmec Indians in Central America probably first used the word cacao around 1000 BC. The Aztecs made 'xocoatl', a bitter drink, flavoured with maize and chillies. Hernán Cortés introduced cacao to Spain in 1528 where it was not well received. Clever cooks started to add sugar and it became popular with the European nobility.

Cacao powder contains more than three times the flavonoids found in green tea. Chocolate is a good source of copper, magnesium and other minerals. It improves blood flow and lowers blood pressure. Its positive effect on blood vessels and cholesterol levels prevents cardiovascular diseases.

Furthermore, cacao improves digestion and stimulates the kidneys. It improves blood flow to the skin. It also improves blood flow to the brain, memory and brain function in elderly people.

A GOOD NIGHT'S SLEEP

Sleeping well at night is vital for a healthy lifestyle. When menopause approached, I woke up almost every night. I read books for one or two hours until my eyes felt heavy. Many times, I could not fall asleep again. I believe that lack of sleep contributed to my depression.

Alcohol hinders restful sleep at night. When you have sleep problems, limit yourself to two or three drinks a day and avoid drinking alcohol three hours before bedtime. I love wine but I stopped drinking in the evening.

When you use wine for baking, like in the following recipe, all alcohol evaporates. I love this cake, a staple in my mother's kitchen. The only word to describe its flavour combination – red wine with chocolate and cinnamon – is 'heavenly'.

78 RED WINE CAKE

My mother covers this cake with a simple sugar frosting made from icing sugar with water. I chose white chocolate as contrast to the dark cake.

INGREDIENTS

(For a 25 cm/10 in round cake dish)

- 🌶 300 ml red wine
- 🌶 200 gm dark chocolate
- 🌶 200 gm butter
- 🌶 2 cups sugar

- 🍳 2 cups whole-wheat flour
- 🍳 6 eggs
- 🍳 2 tbsp baking powder
- 🍳 1 tbsp vanilla extract
- 🍳 2 tbsp cacao
- 🍳 1 tbsp ground cinnamon
- 🍳 300 gm white chocolate

METHOD

Grate dark chocolate with a hand grater. Butter the cake dish.

When I make cakes, I don't cream butter with sugar and then add eggs. It is easier to melt butter; two minutes in the microwave does the trick. Place eggs, sugar and vanilla extract into a bowl and whip with a hand mixer to light yellow cream.

Add grated chocolate, melted butter and wine, and stir. Sieve flour, cacao, cinnamon and baking powder into the bowl, stir and fill into prepared dish.

Bake at 190 degrees Celsius for about fifty minutes. Let it cool down.

Cut white chocolate into pieces and place into a bowl. Melt in the microwave or a double boiler. I microwave chocolate at medium for one minute, and then add another minute if needed. Spread melted chocolate over cake and let it set.

RED WINE – HEALTHY ALCOHOL

Red wine seems to be the healthiest kind of alcoholic drink – but only when consumed in moderation. People who drink one glass of red wine a day reduce their risk of heart disease by a third. Red wine seems to keep the good kinds of cholesterol in the blood stream and reduces the damage done by bad cholesterol. Some experts believe the high content of antioxidants in red wine is responsible for the so-called French paradox. This refers to the fact that French people rarely suffer from heart disease although they eat a lot of saturated fat.

MYSTERIOUS SLUMBER

Scientists cannot answer the question on why we need to sleep. When we don't sleep enough we feel irritable, cannot concentrate and tend to gain weight. A lot of research has only resulted in theories so far.

The energy conservation theory suggests that we sleep to slow down our metabolism and to conserve our energy resources. Some scientists believe that sleep serves to repair our bodies. Muscle growth, tissue repair, protein synthesis and the release of growth hormones happen during sleep. The brain plasticity theory proposes that we sleep so that our brain can reorganize itself and assimilate experiences made during the day. Some experts think the brain uses sleep to connect experiences with emotions and to develop pictures that play out as dreams.

Sometimes I experience wild dreams. Sometimes I wake up angry because I had to fight in my dreams. One would think the brain would be kind enough to keep struggles to our waking hours when we have to deal with them in real life. I never bothered analysing my dreams because most seem random, but I may be wrong.

I have to admit, sometimes I dream about food, especially chocolate. Some time ago, I was baking a chocolate cake in my dreams. When I woke up, I did not just bake any chocolate cake – I made my all-time favourite.

79 CHOCOLATE CAKE

During the more than fifty years of my life, I have come across many chocolate cakes. I cannot stand the commercial kind, chocolate-coloured sponge filled with chocolate cream. Most bakeries use vegetable shortening, a blend of vegetable fats that suffocates your liver and clings to the walls of your arteries.

I am all for rich, chocolatey goodness, but I need first-grade ingredients. I refuse to swallow inferior quality – especially when it comes to sinful delights. This cake does not contain any flour, but plenty of chocolate, nuts, butter and eggs.

INGREDIENTS

(For a 24 cm/9 in springform)

- 250 gm chocolate
- ½ cup cacao
- 1 cup sugar
- 7 eggs
- 200 gm almonds
- ½ cup desiccated coconut flakes
- 175 gm butter
- 5 tbsp homemade vanilla extract (or 1 tbsp commercial extract and 4 tbsp rum)

- Butter to grease the springform
- Baking paper

ICING

- 150 gm dark chocolate
- 50 ml strong coffee
- 50 gm butter

METHOD

Break chocolate into pieces and melt with butter in a double boiler. Stir well and let it cool down.

Cover springform with butter. Spread baking paper over bottom and clip springform together. Cut off any excess paper. Preheat the oven to 160 degrees Celsius.

Place eggs, sugar and vanilla extract into a bowl and stir. Grind almonds and add to bowl with coconut flakes and cacao powder. Stir well.

Add chocolate-butter mixture, stir and fill into form. Bake for around forty-five minutes until just set. The top should show some cracks. Don't overcook it. A toothpick inserted in middle should appear slightly brown. Let it cool down in oven.

Melt chocolate with coffee and butter in a double boiler and mix. Place cake on a platter and cover with icing.

NO FANCY TECHNIQUE

Many recipes for flourless chocolate cakes tell you to beat egg whites to stiff peaks to lighten the mixture. This leads to a cake that rises and collapses – a look that reminds me of broken promises. This recipe does away with fancy technique. You stir the ingredients together and bake them. It rises a bit, but not much. The result is a creamy, incredibly chocolatey cake that melts in your mouth. Because of its sinful calorie content, I substitute lunch with a big piece of this chocolate wonder. I guess it keeps well but I have not had the chance to test this. It always disappears almost immediately.

SUNLIGHT FOR SWEET DREAMS

During premenopause, my mood went into a downside spiral. The more tired I became the worse I felt. I reached a state of emotional exhaustion. I wallowed in depression and did not have the energy to second-guess myself. I thought I was just a bit sad and annoyed. When my gynaecologist prescribed antidepressants, a grey veil lifted and I could feel joy again. I also slept much better.

This antidepressant worked with serotonin. When you increase serotonin levels in the brain, you automatically improve melatonin levels, the hormone that helps us fall asleep. Melatonin controls the body's internal clock, also called circadian rhythms.

Sunlight greatly influences our endocrine system that keeps our hormones balanced. Sunlight tells the pineal gland in the brain to produce less melatonin and more serotonin, the happy-maker that keeps us alert. When you dim the light at night, serotonin turns into melatonin and you fall asleep easily.

On the Internet, I found melatonin described as the 'master hormone' because it controls the body's internal clock. Melatonin also acts as a powerful antioxidant, improving the immune system. I don't think there is a master hormone. Many different substances contribute to our well-being and need to be balanced.

When somebody praises melatonin as a wonder hormone, most likely they sell expensive melatonin pills. Because of the blood-brain barrier it is useless to eat them. Remember, this barrier only allows small building blocks for hormones and neurotransmitters into the brain. Melatonin and serotonin have to be synthesized inside the brain itself. But one should never underestimate the placebo effect.

Many techniques further a good night's sleep without sleeping pills. Dim the lights in the hours before bedtime. Keep your bedroom as dark as possible because this furthers melatonin release. Relax before going to bed—take a bath, read a book or do a bit of meditation. Now is not the time to exercise.

If you did not sleep well during the night, you can catch up with a nap during the day. But avoid napping late afternoon because it might keep you from falling asleep. Stick to a routine: go to sleep and wake up at the same time. Cultivating happy feelings immediately after waking up is important too.

80 MUFFINS

Who doesn't like freshly baked muffins? I love the scent of chocolate muffins, announcing a wonderful breakfast. Nothing beats morning blues better than a muffin fresh from the oven.

INGREDIENTS

(Makes 22 small or 12 big muffins)

- 4 eggs
- 2 cups sugar
- 1 tbsp vanilla essence
- 1 cup cacao powder
- 1 cup cold pressed coconut oil
- 100 gm desiccated coconut flakes
- 3 teaspoons baking soda
- 3 teaspoons baking powder
- 2 cups rolled oats
- 3 cups whole-wheat flour
- 300 ml milk
- Oil and paper lining for the moulds
- Icing sugar for dusting the muffins

METHOD

Grease muffin moulds and line with paper. Preheat oven to 190 degrees Celsius. Crack eggs in a bowl, add vanilla essence and sugar, and stir. Sift cacao powder over mixture, add coconut flakes, coconut oil, milk and mix. Blend baking powder, soda and oats with flour, add to bowl and mix.

Fill muffin moulds and bake for twenty-five minutes, finishing with five minutes of grill. If you use big moulds, bake for five more minutes in the oven. Dust with icing sugar.

SATURATED FATS PLAY A VITAL ROLE

Saturated fats still suffer from a negative image, which dates back to the latter half of the previous century. Saturated fats were held responsible for the increase of heart disease in the USA, condemning butter as well as coconut oil. Polyunsaturated vegetable oils were considered healthy.

In recent years, many experts have made a complete turnaround. Polyunsaturated vegetable oils may be the bad guys. These fats are alien to our bodies that cannot digest them properly. However, they are cheap and convenient for the food industry. One of the first doctors to warn about the dangers of vegetable oils was Weston Price. He published several books about nutrition. Some called him a visionary pioneer and others condemned him as a quack.

Coconut oil was wrongly condemned by public opinion too. This oil has been rediscovered lately. I love it for baking sweets. In *Coconut Diet*, author Cherie Calbom claims that saturated fats like butter and coconut oil are vital for the human body (the following points are taken from *Coconut Diet*):

- A big part of cell membranes are made from saturated fatty acids.
- Our bones need saturated fatty acids to incorporate calcium.
- Saturated fatty acids protect the liver and enhance the immune system.
- Tissues absorb omega-3 fatty acids better when consumed with saturated fat.

CHOCOLATE LOVER'S DELIGHT

In recent years, culinary culture in Goa improved greatly. The first place with French cuisine was a French restaurant around twenty years ago. After a few years, the three French owners moved to Ashvem where they started La Plage, one of the best beach shacks in Goa. It is our favourite place to enjoy the beach.

Our son loves their molten chocolate cake. Once I asked about the recipe. I was told that this adapted French recipe relies on exact measurements. This impressed me so much that I did not dare to prepare this dessert.

Then a pizza chain put chocolate lava cake on the menu. They were tiny, cost a fortune and came with a gooey centre – if you were lucky. I felt taken for a ride. I don't mind paying big money for good food but I want to see something on my plate. Tiny bits don't do it for me, especially when it comes to chocolate.

81 MOLTEN LAVA CAKE

For the sake of texture, I used to beat eggs with sugar to a rather firm cream. One day, I felt lazy and just stirred eggs, sugar and flour together by hand and then added the chocolate-butter mixture. The result turned out beautifully.

INGREDIENTS

(For 4 ramekins of 175 ml)

🍴 120 gm dark chocolate

- 🍴 100 gm butter
- 🍴 ½ cup icing sugar
- 🍴 ¼ cup flour
- 🍴 3 eggs
- 🍴 2 tbsp homemade vanilla essence
- 🍴 Butter to grease the ramekins

METHOD

Preheat oven to 190 degrees Celsius. Break chocolate into pieces and melt with butter in a double boiler. Stir well.

Butter ramekins. Break eggs into a bowl. Add icing sugar and vanilla essence, and stir. Add flour and melted chocolate, and combine. Fill ramekins.

Bake for ten to fifteen minutes.

The baking time is crucial and depends on experience. The top of the cakes should just set and the middle should remain soft. In my gas oven, I bake them for eight minutes in the middle of the oven and then give them two minutes from the grill to solidify the top. Serve immediately.

CHOCO LAVA CAKE: A MODERN DESSERT

Every chocolate enthusiast knows what a choco lava cake is all about: a deliciously soft centre. Choco lava cakes conquered the world just a few years ago. Our cakes date back to the French chef Michel Bras, who patented his chocolate coulant in 1981. This cake had a centre of chocolate ganache and was frozen overnight before baking. In 1987, Jean-Georges Vongerichten reinvented the molten chocolate cake in New

York by accident. He pulled a chocolate sponge cake, made with his mother's recipe, too early from the oven – and then discovered how delicious it was.

SLEEP APPS AND SNACKS

Thanks to anti-depressants, I slept well again and I realized that the lack of sleep had made me completely apathetic. As a former journalist, I believe in information and research. Whenever I encounter something that I don't understand, I turn to books and the Internet to remedy my ignorance.

Today, countless apps wait to be discovered. I recommend guided meditations and sleep-inducing sounds. When you wake up at night, try to fall asleep again by just lying still. If this is not possible, try a sleep app, read a book and eat a little something. A little snack in the middle of the night can put you back into the arms of Morpheus.

The following recipe offers a great snack for sleepless night hours because you can keep it in the fridge for several days: chocolate mousse. The traditional recipe includes raw eggs, making it a risky concoction.

82 CHOCOLATE MOUSSE

The original recipe deals with 200 grams of chocolate. This amount seemed ridiculously small considering my two chocoholics in the house. I use 500 grams, which gives you eight generous servings.

INGREDIENTS

(Serves 8)

- 500 gm chocolate (either dark or milk chocolate)
- 200 ml cream
- 150 ml strong coffee, best mocha or espresso
- 1 tbsp vanilla essence
- Ice

☞ TIP: You can replace the cream with coconut or almond milk if you are allergic to dairy products.

METHOD

You need a large amount of ice. I fill a stainless steel bowl with water and freeze it overnight. When needed, I break it into pieces by breaking it with a hammer. Then I place ice pieces into a bowl, add water and refrigerate.

Cut chocolate into pieces; melt with cream, vanilla essence and coffee in a double boiler.

Take bowl with ice water, pour melted chocolate into a bowl and place it into ice water. Whisk this mixture with an electric hand mixer.

After a few minutes, the chocolate should thicken. When you have a creamy mousse, you are done. This should not take longer than 10 minutes.

If the mousse remains runny, you have used too much liquid. Add some chocolate pieces to mixture; melt and whip again in the ice bath.

DISCOVERING MOUSSE

In my quest for safe chocolate mousse, I discovered Heston Blumenthal's recipe for Chocolate Chantilly, a fine example of molecular gastronomy, and a branch of cooking quite alien to me. The simplicity of the recipe convinced me. It relies on a temperature shock for the melted chocolate while whipping.

Naturally, a lot can go wrong. My first attempt ended in disaster with chocolate drops all over the counter, the walls and myself. My second attempt went well so I am happy to share it with you. I use less liquid than Heston and I have replaced water with a mixture of cream and coffee.

HEALTHY APPROACH TO WORRIES

Sometimes I feel scared for my son. When kids are small, danger seems to lurk around every corner. In his teenage years, the dangers seem to increase. But I don't want to put the weight of my worries on the shoulders of my son. I try to remember that worries are problems in the future and we should deal with them when they arise.

I have a sticker next to my computer with the words 'No Fear', reminding me to stick to a healthy attitude. During psychotherapy, I had encouraging slogans plastered all over my apartment. 'Everything is love' was written on the boiler in the bathroom. 'You can do what you want' graced the fridge door. 'Don't worry, be happy' greeted me in my cupboard.

I believe it is normal to worry, nothing wrong with that. But we should keep our worries to ourselves. Parents have to accept that our worries should not burden our children.

I encourage my son to follow his dreams, no matter what. I have followed dreams all my life despite financial insecurity. Money is not everything, although it may seem so. My family has absolute priority. That's why I don't mind spending many hours in the kitchen. But I don't want to be a slave to cooking. I like to have a stash in the freezer and a cookie jar filled with home-baked snacks.

The following recipe for chocolate cookies provides mood-lifting snacks. Two cookies should fill your belly and keep you going. They contain a lot of nuts and plenty of oats.

83 CHOCOLATE COOKIES

Super easy to prepare, chocolate cookies can be prepared anytime, anywhere. This requires very few ingredients and you can experiment with the basic recipe in your own way.

INGREDIENTS

(Makes 24)

- 6 eggs
- 2½ cups sugar
- 1 cup cacao powder
- 1 tbsp vanilla essence
- 200 gm fresh, grated coconut (about 1 coconut)
- 200 gm walnuts
- 5 cups oats
- 1 cup whole wheat flour
- 200 gm butter
- Grease for the cookie sheets

METHOD

Grate coconut flesh. Chop walnuts roughly. Spread butter over two cookie sheets. Break eggs into a bowl. Add sugar and vanilla essence, and stir. Add cacao powder, soft butter, coconut flakes and walnuts, and mix. Add oats and flour, and stir again.

Place heaps on the cookie sheets. One standard size cookie sheet holds twelve cookies, three rows of four.

Bake at 190 degrees Celsius for twenty-five minutes.

THE GO-TO SNACK

This recipe can be changed easily according to the ingredients in your pantry. You can use coconut oil or butter. You can use any kind of nuts. You can use any kind of sweetener you like. Just keep roughly to the amounts given in the recipe. Of course you cannot substitute the cacao powder if you want chocolate cookies.

The baking time is crucial. They should remain soft and chewy in the centre. Every oven bakes differently so you need to rely on your experience.

I use a gas oven, which is probably the worst oven for baking sweets. The heat comes only from the bottom. You have to be careful that your sweets are not burning from below while remaining raw on the top. That's why I always end baking sweets with a few minutes under the grill.

MONEY PLAYS A MINOR ROLE

In recent years, scientists of many areas have started to research happiness. The official scientific name for happiness is 'subjective well-being' (SWB). Scientists agree that genes determine about 50 per cent of our disposition to happiness. That leaves ample room for improvement. Experts conclude that we can raise our levels of happiness by practising a happiness-furthering lifestyle. Good sleep, regular exercise and optimistic outlook contribute to happy emotions.

Interestingly, money plays only a minor role in attaining happiness. Many studies have researched the relationship between income and personal happiness. As long as we have enough for middle-class comfort, a raise in income does almost nothing. Relationships on the other hand are important. We need close connections, intimate relationships; the embrace of love, in whatever forms it comes along.

For me, chocolate truffles are a kind of eatable love. Many times, people ask me if they can order my truffles but they are not for sale. You can only get my truffles for free. You need to be family or friend. There are some things in life money can't buy and my truffles belong to them.

84 TRUFFLES

Nothing gets chocoholics more hooked than homemade truffles. I don't make them all the time, only for Christmas because I don't follow the German tradition of Christmas cookies. My mother still bakes around fifteen different kinds every year. I could never bake them as good as she does.

But I don't want my men missing special sweets on Christmas. The weeks before Christmas, truffles reign supreme in my kitchen. Last year I made 750 truffles and they were all gone by the end of January. I like to give them away to friends for Christmas. My men watch jealously how many truffles leave the house.

MOCHA TRUFFLES

INGREDIENTS

(Makes 24)

- 400 gm dark chocolate
- 4 tbsp butter
- 100 ml cream
- 4 tbsp whiskey
- 6 tbsp mocha, espresso or very strong Nescafé
- 1 cup sifted cacao powder

METHOD

Melt chopped chocolate with butter, cream, coffee and whiskey in a double boiler. Stir chocolate mixture until you have smooth cream.

Refrigerate until mixture has set. Be careful that it does not turn too hard. You need to be able to form balls.

Roll balls between palms of your hand and coat with sifted cacao powder.

Store truffles in a closed container in fridge.

☞ **TIP:** If you are not a fan of dark chocolate, use milk chocolate for this recipe, double the amount of cream and omit the butter. Instead of whiskey you can also use brandy or any other kind of liquor.

How many truffles you manage to get out of the given amount depends upon the size you are making. I make mine quite big.

WHITE CHOCOLATE TRUFFLES

INGREDIENTS

(Makes 24)

- 150 gm almonds
- 4 tbsp cream
- 5 tbsp butter
- 1 cup sugar
- 1 cup icing sugar
- 300 gm white chocolate
- Butter for cookie sheet

> ☞ **TIP:** Making caramel is dangerous. Keep a bowl with ice water nearby. Never add salt to dry caramel! I tried this one time and the caramel got madly out of control. It bubbled over the pan, all over my oven and onto the floor. I spent hours scraping it off.

METHOD

Bring two glasses of water to a boil. Soak almonds for ten minutes. Drain and remove skins. Toast in oven at lowest temperature until golden brown. Chop toasted almonds roughly and place on a buttered cookie sheet.

Place sugar in a pan with heavy bottom over medium heat and caramelize. When it has turned golden-copper in colour, spread over almonds. When it is set, break caramel into big pieces and chop roughly.

Melt white chocolate with butter and cream in a double boiler and combine. Stir almonds into chocolate and place into fridge until firm. Form small balls and roll in icing sugar.

COCONUT TRUFFLES

INGREDIENTS

(Makes 24)

- 150 gm desiccated coconut flakes
- ½ tin (200 gm) sweetened, condensed milk
- 2 tbsp vanilla essence
- 2 tbsp brandy
- 300 gm dark chocolate
- 4 tbsp butter

METHOD

Place coconut, condensed milk, brandy and vanilla essence into a bowl and mix. Refrigerate until mixture has set.

Melt roughly-chopped chocolate with butter in a double boiler and stir.

Roll coconut mix into balls.

With help of a fork, dip balls into melted chocolate and let set on a sheet of aluminium foil.

PEANUT BUTTER TRUFFLES

INGREDIENTS

(Makes 24)

- 300 gm milk chocolate
- 100 gm peanut butter
- 50 gm tahini (sesame paste)
- 300 ml cream
- 5 tbsp butter
- 2 tbsp vanilla essence
- 2 cups roasted peanuts

METHOD

Place peanuts on a cookie sheet and roast at lowest temperature in oven.

Let peanuts cool down. Remove skins and roughly chop peanuts in a blender.

Melt chopped chocolate with peanut butter, tahini, cream, butter and vanilla essence in a double boiler and combine. Refrigerate until mixture has set. Form small balls and roll them in chopped peanuts.

> ☞ TIP: I coat these truffles in roasted peanuts. You could also use cacao powder, icing sugar, chopped roasted almonds or desiccated coconut flakes.

FIRST AID WHEN CHOCOLATE SPLITS

Probably you won't have a problem when you prepare truffles in the given amounts of my recipes. However, when you want to make bigger amounts things can get hairy. When you notice that the chocolate ganache turns shiny and oil starts oozing out, your mixture has split.

Luckily, a split ganache is easy to fix. Grab an electric hand mixer and start beating on high speed. Sometimes this immediate action is enough to save your mixture.

If not, grab some cream (or milk) and stir it into the mixture. One or two packets of cream so far saved every ganache I have made. Remember to act quickly when you notice that the mixture splits. The sooner you administer first aid, the easier it is to save your ganache.

CHOCOLATE AS HAPPY MAKERS

Chocolate makes everybody happy. I think few people will deny this fact. Scientists still try to pinpoint the ways in which chocolate affects us. Various theories and results of studies make rounds on the Internet. One researcher in San Diego discovered that chocolate has a similar effect like marijuana by inhibiting the breakdown of anandamide in the brain. Anandamide is a recently discovered happy-making neurotransmitter. Other scientists state that the anti-depressant phenylethylalanine, found in chocolate, is responsible for its happy-making qualities.

Honestly, I don't care. However, I cannot help feeling a slight mistrust towards people who don't appreciate chocolate. Forgive me if you belong to these strange individuals. I have made the experience that few gifts are as well received as homemade chocolates, especially truffles. Give it a try!

CHAPTER 8

KITCHEN MUST-HAVES

As a housewife, I like to be prepared for emergencies like unexpected guests. A well-stocked freezer helps when you have to rustle up a dinner quickly. I always keep two or three pasta sauces ready. In case I don't feel like cooking, dinner can be served with minimum effort. Taking care of your own happiness includes cutting yourself some slack. We are not robots. There are days when we don't function well.

Some basic concoctions greatly ease your life as a cook and provider of healthy, hearty family meals. In this chapter I have compiled the recipes for dishes that I like to have in stock.

Garlic butter – or any kind of scented butter – can be used in many different ways. You can even dress pasta with it. Onion jam is another fabulous recipe. I describe its taste as fried onions on steroids; you can keep it in the fridge for weeks. Intense chicken stock enlivens every recipe, an essential element in my freezer.

Homemade curd and paneer many times make a huge difference in a recipe. My tzatziki would not taste as nice with store-bought yoghurt. Cheesecake turns out better when prepared with your own, creamy paneer.

Real vanilla essence is made in no time at all and tastes far superior than commercial stuff. Caramel and sweet sauces deliver the wow factor in a few minutes. Fruits in alcohol are a staple in my fridge too.

Many times, these simple basic dishes have helped me woo my guests without slaving in the kitchen. I don't consider it a virtue to sacrifice the biggest part of your time for the sake of family and friends. I am a modern woman. I pursue many interests and cooking is only one of them.

POWER OF SMELL

Nothing can invoke memories like smell. The olfactory impact of food is as important as its taste. Nuances of taste are provoked by smell. When food enters our mouth, its smell travels through the retro nasal canal into the brain where the olfactory bulb registers it as taste.

One of my favourite aromas is sizzling garlic. It instantly takes me back to happy childhood days in a French village. My father's mother was born in Alsace, along the south-west border of Germany with France. Vineyards, old villages and green forests dot this countryside. Although German blood flows through the veins of Alsatians, they lean towards French culinary culture.

When I was a child, my parents visited our relatives in Alsace – owners of a vineyard – at least once a year to stock up on fine wines. We stayed with our aunt Marie in Mittelbergheim, a village with crooked streets and old houses perched on top of a hill. Aunt Marie would traditionally serve dinner starting with snails in garlic butter, followed by a rabbit – either stewed or roasted. I use garlic butter mostly to make crunchy garlic bread.

85 GARLIC BUTTER

You can always find a container of garlic butter in my fridge because it is so versatile. I can produce a tray of garlic bread in a few minutes; use it as condiment for pasta or substitute garlic in a recipe. I serve crunchy garlic bread as an appetizer with cheese or dips like hummus, tzatziki or baba ghanoush. You can store it up to one month in the fridge.

You can prepare scented butter in many different ways. For example, lemon butter made with lemon zest and parsley or chilly butter with garlic, ginger and finely chopped fresh red chillies. It is important to finely chop the aromatics to infuse the butter.

INGREDIENTS

- 500 gm salted butter
- 2 bunches parsley, preferably flat-leaf parsley
- 1 big head garlic

METHOD

Please don't stick to given amounts. All my recipes can be used as guidelines. Vary them according to taste and ingredients available. Flat-leaf parsley can be substituted with normal parsley or coriander.

Use butter at room temperature to blend easily. Chop parsley and garlic finely. Mix parsley and garlic with butter and place in an airtight container.

GARLIC BREAD – THE BEST USE OF GARLIC BUTTER

You can prepare garlic bread from any kind of bread. The amount of bread depends on the number of people you want to serve. I calculate two big or four small slices per head.

Slice bread; toast one side on a cookie sheet in oven at lowest temperature. Turn slices around so toasted side is on top. Spread garlic butter over it and toast again. Garlic bread is ready when the bread has turned golden brown around the edges.

ELUSIVE STATE OF HAPPINESS

When I started writing this book, defining happiness seemed like the logical point to begin. Then I began to think and think, and I am still wondering what happiness exactly means. I believe happiness means many things to many people. Each of us has to find his or her own path. Happiness is a moment of bliss, elusive yet often attainable if you know how to look for it.

I believe in subjectivity. The often-praised objectivity is a myth – even in journalism. We can try to communicate objectively verifiable facts and, for me, that is as far as objectivity goes. As human beings we are subjective; we are individuals.

Can I know how chocolate tastes in your mouth? I cannot.

I can only know how it tastes in mine. Obviously our senses work in a similar way because many people love chocolate. We all live in our own universe defined by our experiences and the perceptions of our senses.

One trait of my universe is the knowledge I have gained about food and its many implications on our body, mind and soul. I have reached a point where I can truly enjoy the food on my plate and I know how to produce it.

Some things add instant delight to any dish, like onion jam. Done correctly, its flavours explode in your mouth. Imagine the aroma of fried onions exponentially multiplied.

86 ONION JAM

Onion jam is easy to prepare. The only danger is burning the jam; that's why you should keep an eye on it during the final stages of cooking. The first time I made onion jam, I almost burnt it. One minute more and it would have been a disaster. Luck was on my side that day.

INGREDIENTS

(Serves 8)

- 1 kg onions
- 3 tbsp butter, ghee or oil
- 6 tbsp sugar
- 1 tsp salt
- Water

METHOD

Peel onions and slice finely with a food processor. Heat butter, oil or ghee in a pan with a thick bottom and a tight-fitting lid, and add onions. There should not be any sizzling when they hit the pan. Dribble sugar and salt over onions, and stir. Add 200 millilitres water and mix.

When contents in the pan are too hot to touch, put flame as low as possible. If you have a heat diffuser, use it.

Close the pan with lid and simmer for an hour. Onion slices should be soft at this point.

Keep on simmering for at least one more hour. Check regularly every ten to fifteen minutes.

Onion jam is ready when liquid has evaporated and onions have turned dark bronze. Colour changes during last stage of cooking. At this point it needs your constant attention. Keep stirring onion jam every few minutes after it has passed the two hour mark.

You can keep onion jam in fridge for two weeks.

☞ TIP: The original recipe calls for Marsala wine or other sweet wine. I have substituted wine with water and sugar, which works well for me.

BEST ACCOMPANIMENT

Onion jam tastes wonderful with chicken liver pâté. One vegetarian friend of mine enjoys it simply on buttered toast.

PURSUIT OF HAPPINESS

Philosophers have come up with many descriptions of happiness. Aristotle, the man of the golden mean, formulated around 350 BC that happiness is the ultimate purpose of the human existence. He defined the way to happiness as the exercise of virtues like courage, generosity and friendship. At the same time, Mencius preached a similar concept to the kings of China caught up in a war for power. He urged them to follow their 'sprouts' of virtue deep inside. About 200 years earlier, Confucius had taught that one could achieve happiness by learning about human relationships.

Around 1250 AD, the Christian thinker Thomas Aquinas stated that perfect happiness belongs in heaven when we meet God face to face. Human beings could only attain imperfect happiness on earth by contemplating truth. His teachings are similar to the writings of Abu Hamid al-Ghazali, an Islamic theologist, who lived about 100 years before Aquinas. He writes that happiness comes from self-knowledge linked to the knowledge of God.

The English philosopher John Locke coined the phrase 'pursuit of happiness' in 1689. He writes that the necessity of pursuing happiness is the foundation of liberty. Locke's philosophy influenced the French Revolution. Thomas Jefferson also implemented the right to life, liberty and pursuit of happiness into the American Declaration of Independence.

For me, writing cookbooks enhances my life. I can share my daily experiences with many people. Few things state accomplishment like your name printed on a book cover – I am sure that I leave a legacy for my son.

Like every ambitious home cook, I know about the importance of stock. For years I wanted to make stock in my kitchen, but I just could not muster the energy to prepare something that I could buy. That changed when I deboned two huge chickens and stuffed them, turning them into a galantine or ballotine, like the French call them. I was left with a mountain of chicken bones and wings – time to make chicken stock. Heston Blumenthal's method convinced me. When it comes to chicken stock, I think he nails it.

87 CHICKEN STOCK

The perfectionist Blumenthal goes overboard with his directions also for chicken stock. He takes two kilograms of chicken wings and adds seventy-five grams of carrot and 150 grams of onions; both 'peeled and finely sliced'. Give me a break, dear Heston! I am supposed to peel and finely slice carrots and onions and then weigh them? Not in my kitchen.

I make do with taking one medium carrot and one big onion. It works just fine. Maybe not for Heston's illustrious taste buds, but mine accept this crude way of cooking. I prefer measuring cups to balancing exactly. Many times I wing amounts by feeling. I heavily reduce this stock to a syrupy concentrate that I freeze in ice cube moulds.

INGREDIENTS

(Makes 300 ml concentrated stock)

- 2 kg chicken pieces
- 1 carcass from roast chicken
- 6 tbsp milk powder
- 1 big onion
- 1 medium carrot
- 100 gm white button mushrooms
- 2 big garlic cloves

☞ **TIP:** If you don't have a leftover carcass from a roast chicken, don't worry. Although it would be desirable, the recipe works without it.

METHOD

Preheat oven to 200 degrees Celsius. Place chicken pieces on a cookie sheet and sprinkle milk powder over them. Roast for one hour. Turn every twenty minutes to ensure caramelizing without burning.

Clean and chop onions and carrot. Rinse mushrooms and quarter. Add to cookie sheet and brown them. Place browned chicken pieces into pressure cooker together with carcass, vegetables and garlic.

Pour warm water onto cookie sheet and scrape away all browned, caramelized bits. Add this water to pressure cooker. If needed, add some more water until you have reached maximum water level. Cook for two hours on low flame after first whistle.

Drain liquid through sieve into a normal pot and reduce to thick syrup. Fill into ice cube trays and freeze.

CHICKEN STOCK FOR EXTRA FLAVOUR

Chicken stock cubes add a little bit of extra flavour to many dishes. Commercial stock cubes are loaded with preservatives and taste enhancers so I avoid them. I always put stock into my risottos and sautéed vegetables. Frozen stock also injects extra roasted aroma into curries and other dishes with a sauce.

FORMULA FOR PERFECT BREAKFAST

The first hour of the day can decide if you greet the world with open arms or if you feel miserable. Cultivate a morning routine that eases your way into the day. There is no solution that fits all. I need gentle nursing with coffee in the morning. Luckily, my husband willingly prepares coffee for me – an excellent one too, I might add, Italian style mocha.

When you wake up, your body has not had anything to eat for some hours. If you skip breakfast, you set your body up for cravings. In her book *Eat Your Way to Happiness*, Elizabeth Somer writes about her 1-2-3 rules for breakfast. She recommends one to three servings of high quality carbohydrates, two servings of fruit or vegetables and one serving of protein.

Although it might sound complicated, it is easy to achieve. One example of a perfect breakfast would be a whole-wheat or multigrain roll, topped with slices of tomato and cheese, turkey or ham and a piece of fruit like an apple or orange or half a papaya. A bowl of oatmeal with milk and fruits or rotis with bhaji and milk fit the bill.

In the evenings I clean and wash fruits and vegetables. In my pantry, I always store cereal, toppings and nuts. Luckily, my men don't expect elaborate breakfast dishes.

It is important to eat complex carbohydrates in the morning, delivered by whole grains and legumes. These carbohydrates replenish glucose that has been used during the night. Protein and fibre give you staying power, slow down digestion and make you feel full. Fruits or vegetables deliver vitamins and antioxidants, helping your body to cope with free radicals.

One of my favourite dairy products – and ideal as part of the perfect breakfast – is full-fat Greek yoghurt. Although India provides a wealth of dairy products, super rich curd has not made it yet onto the shelves. That's why I have started to experiment with homemade dairy products.

88 BE YOUR OWN DAIRY QUEEN

In the beginning, I tried to remove water from store-bought curd by hanging it. I started to make curd by mixing milk with curd and then hung it, but it never reached the perfect consistency. Thanks to a culinary epiphany, I used cream instead of milk and it worked. After hanging curd for three hours it comes pretty close to rich Greek stuff – with little effort.

The other dairy item I find useful to make at home is paneer. This ricotta-like cheese is done in a few minutes.

Homemade paneer tastes better and is creamier than store-bought one. You only need to remember a few rules: Don't add the curdling agent when the milk is boiling. Let it cool down a few minutes. Don't stir it vigorously; touch it as gently as possible for a creamy texture. Don't overdo the pressing. The result is worth the effort.

When I make cheesecake, I use equal amounts of hung curd and paneer. The amounts yielded by the recipe can vary depending on the type of milk you use. I always work with milk and cream from tetra pack because it is easier to handle than fresh milk.

INGREDIENTS

YOGHURT

(Makes 3 cups)

- 1 litre cream
- 100 ml curd
- Clean cotton cloth

METHOD

Place cream into container and whisk well with curd. Cover container with lid but don't close it. Curd needs air to develop. Keep overnight in a warm place.

Pour curd onto a big, clean cloth. Tie ends of cloth together and secure with rubber band or rope. Hang curd, preferably over a sink. Let it drip for three hours or until dripping has stopped. Store in fridge.

PANEER

(Makes 2 cups)

- 1 litre milk
- 200 ml cream
- ½ cup of water
- Pinch of salt
- ¼ cup synthetic vinegar or lemon/lime juice
- Clean cotton cloth

> ☞ TIP: I prefer synthetic vinegar for making paneer because the taste vanishes and I don't have to squeeze lemons or lime.

METHOD

Place water in a pot with a heavy bottom. When water has heated up, add milk. After some time, add cream and stir well. Add a good pinch of salt.

Bring milk to a bubble; let it cool down for a few minutes.

Add synthetic vinegar or lemon/lime juice. Wait a bit and then nudge gently. Whey should turn light green and separate immediately from curdled milk. If whey looks white or nothing much is happening, add tablespoons of vinegar or lemon/lime juice until milk curdles.

Pour curdled milk into a colander lined with cloth. Gently squeeze out excess liquid and hang paneer for eight minutes. The dripping should stop. Press between two plates with a weight on top for half an hour.

PANEER: PROTEINS FOR VEGETARIANS

Many vegetarians rely on milk products like paneer to consume enough proteins. Paneer delivers proteins in a way that can be used in many dishes. I use it as fresh cheese in my cheesecake but I also love the typical Indian dish, palak paneer. Vegetarians can add grilled paneer cubes to salads to turn them into a complete yet light meal. You can also include grated paneer in many cake batters, for example, in a simple sponge cake, to impart extra moisture.

NOTHING EQUALS THE REAL THING

Substitutes rarely make the mark. You cannot experience the feeling of Manhattan skyscrapers by looking at pictures. Dramas on television, although we enjoy them, cannot replace a happy family life.

For years, I have used artificial vanilla extract. Two decades ago, you could not get vanilla beans in Goa. Luckily, the local spice farms have remedied this lack of supply.

Nothing equals real vanilla: its dark brown pods harbour flavour that attracts men like moths. Studies show smelling vanilla arouses most men. It is not clear if the arousal is sexual or culinary in nature. To have the aroma of vanilla pods available at all times, I make my own vanilla essence.

89 PURE AROMA

Vanilla essence is much easier to use than real vanilla beans. You just stir the essence into your dish. You don't need to slice or scrape the vanilla beans. You don't need to heat milk or cream and wait that vanilla seeds infuse the liquid. Because pure food-grade alcohol is not available in India, I go for vodka. Brandy or pure cane liquor also work.

INGREDIENTS

(Makes 200 ml)

- 200 ml vodka, brandy, cane liquor or pure food grade alcohol
- 3 vanilla pods
- 1 bottle with a tight-fitting cap or seal

METHOD

Wash bottle and let it dry. Slit open vanilla pods and place in bottle. Fill with alcohol. Make sure vanilla pods are completely covered. Place bottle in cool, dark place. After two months, vanilla extract is ready for use.

> ☞ **TIP:** Homemade vanilla extract is a great gift for your near and dear ones. The only ingredients you need are pretty glass bottles, alcohol and vanilla.

VANILLA FOR SWEET DELIGHTS

Vanilla is the cardamom for sweets in the western world. Hardly any sweet dish does not include vanilla. This taste is essential for creamy desserts like panna cotta and crème brûlée but it also deepens the flavour of any cake, for example, apple pie, sponge and crumbles. Even truffles depend on the wonderful flavour of vanilla.

DIFFERENCE IN DETAILS

Details often make a huge difference – especially when it comes to desserts. As a German, I enjoy Kaffee und Kuchen (coffee and cake) in the afternoon or as dessert, but we serve just that.

Other nations treat their cakes differently. They don't serve just cake, they deliver it, sometimes chilled, with a sauce and ice cream on the side. In my home, I don't aspire to dish up desserts like in restaurants. Plating up with negative space, a crumble here and a drop of sauce there is not my thing. I leave this to professional chefs.

But I have learnt. Nowadays, I don't serve only ice cream; I offer it with sauce, rum raisins and roasted nuts. I try to think of something to go with a cake, usually a sweet sauce. Also puddings like panna cotta and crème brûlée improve with something on the side. Luckily, it is easy to prepare sweet sauces.

90 SWEET SAUCES

You can indulge in complicated versions of sweet sauces. I consider this unnecessary. You need good ingredients, booze and sugar, that's it. For example, I make chocolate sauce with melted chocolate, milk or cream, espresso coffee and – for adults – dashes of liquor like kahlua, whiskey or cognac. Berries make good fruit sauces but you can use any kind of fruit. The trick is to macerate fruits for at least two hours: clean the fruits, chop them and mix them with sugar and/or liquor. Port wine or cognac is great for strawberries. You get the drift: anything works. Take what you have and throw it together. Not much can go wrong. Be careful not to add too much sugar. You can always put more later.

INGREDIENTS

(Serves 8)

CHOCOLATE SAUCE

- 200 gm chocolate
- 100 ml cream or milk
- 3 tbsp strong coffee
- 2 tbsp liquor

BUTTERSCOTCH SAUCE

- 125 gm butter
- 1 cup brown sugar
- 200 ml cream

FRUIT SAUCE

- 500 gm fruit
- 1 tbsp lemon juice
- 4 tbsp icing sugar
- 50 ml liquor

☞ **TIP:** These are basic recipes. Please understand them as guidelines for your creativity.

METHODS

For chocolate sauce: Chop chocolate into pieces. Melt in a double boiler or microwave with cream or milk, coffee and/or liquor. Stir until you have a smooth sauce. You can make this in advance and just heat up before serving.

For butterscotch sauce: Melt butter in a saucepan, add brown sugar and cream and bring to a boil. Simmer until sugar has dissolved and cream has thickened. Customize sauce with salt, bourbon or scotch, rum or vanilla essence.

For fruit sauce: Clean fruit and cut into pieces. Mix with lemon juice, icing sugar and liquor. Place in container and refrigerate for two hours. When needed, puree fruit. If you use dried fruit, add more liquid and macerate overnight.

SWEET SAUCES GO THE EXTRA MILE

With a sweet sauce you prepare a wonderful dessert in no time at all. Simple vanilla icecream, or any other kind of ice cream, turns into something special when you add a sweet sauce. Also creams like panna cotta improve a lot with a matching sauce. When you have surprise guests, take a store-bought sponge cake and serve it with a dollop of ice cream and a sweet sauce stored in your fridge to make a lasting impression as a gifted chef.

RISING ABOVE FEAR

Emotions cause many events in our daily lives. Remember that feelings are stronger than rational thoughts. Impulses from the limbic system override rational thoughts from the cortex. If one can believe intelligence tests, I am gifted in the brainy department. That does not hinder me to behave like an idiot in the grip of emotions. I can turn into a furious monster if somebody incenses my wrath.

I have inherited this trait from my father who terrified me as a child. When I embarked on my personal overhaul at the age of thirty, I did two things to overcome fear: fire walking and bungee jumping. Fire walking did not pose a real challenge but bungee scared me to death. Never again have I been that scared. Luckily, I was writing a story for my newspaper so I could not chicken out. Somehow I let go and I dropped. My posture could have been better but I did it.

After the jump, I felt ecstatic. If you want to overcome fear of death, I recommend bungee jumping. Just recently, I managed to overcome another fear, this time in the kitchen: dry caramel. Many years ago, I had burnt the skin of my hand with caramel. For the sake of white truffles, I had to deal with my fear.

91 CARAMEL SAUCE

You need a pan with a heavy bottom that distributes heat evenly. Don't use a pan with a dark coating because you need to see the colour. The pan needs to be spotlessly clean; caramel magnifies any impurities. For best results use refined, white sugar. I don't give amounts because that depends on what you want to do with the caramel. To make praline with nuts, take equal amounts of sugar and nuts.

INGREDIENT

🍃 Sugar

METHOD

Spread sugar in an even layer over bottom of pan. Place over medium to low heat and wait.

You need to invoke melting process by gently heating sugar crystals. If heat is too high, sugar will burn at the bottom before it has melted.

Keep checking edges of the sugar where it meets pan. After some minutes edges turn transparent. That means melting has started. When edges have turned golden, gently nudge sugar from border into middle of pan. If colour changes quickly, lower heat. Make sure all sugar crystals have melted by gently moving them. Slowly by slowly all crystals should disappear.

How dark you want your caramel depends on your taste. Lately, I have heard many people raving about taking caramel beyond the smoking point: after melting and turning copper in colour there is a moment when it releases a bit of smoke.

I think this is taking it too far. The hot pan will continue to cook the caramel if you don't plunge it immediately into an ice bath. Even a few seconds too long can turn a great caramel into a burnt mess.

Many people don't like caramel taken to the extreme –

no matter what all the chefs on TV say. However, caramel for white truffles needs to be quite dark. Sniffing it helps. If you detect burnt sugar, discard the caramel. Sugar is not so expensive.

ONE SAUCE, MANY USES

The difference between dry and wet caramel is water. Wet caramel is sugar dissolved in water and then caramelized. Dry caramel is sugar melted in a pan. I was never happy with wet caramel for my white truffles. The sugar solution bubbled so much that it was difficult to see the colour of the caramel. Then I discovered David Lebovitz on the Internet. He describes beautifully how to make dry caramel. Finally, I understood the finer points of melting sugar. The important thing is to use a heavy bottomed pan and to stir gently.

Caramel can be used in many different ways. You can turn it quickly into a sauce, you can spread it over ice cream and you can use it to cover profiteroles. You can coat apples with it and turn nuts into a praline. The best of all: to make caramel you only need sugar, an ingredient that most of us have all the time in the house.

HAPPY MEMORIES

Many happy memories of my childhood days are connected with family feasts. One of my late father's specialities was Rumtopf, literally translated, 'rum pot'. This name describes a big ceramic pot covered by a tight-fitting lid that holds at least five litres. I think my father's Rumtopf contained about ten litres.

Over the course of a year, he placed fruits of the season with sugar and high percentage rum into the pot. The Rumtopf was kept in our pantry and only opened to add more fruits, sugar and rum. This method of preserving fruits in alcohol dates back several hundreds of years and was practised all over Europe.

On Christmas day, my father finally revealed the result of his labour. After the roast turkey, we all shared vanilla ice cream with a generous helping of Rumtopf fruit. I remember lifting myself from the Christmas lunch table in a state of exalted wonderment doubting if my feet would carry me to my bed. After one or two hours' rest, we would meet again, this time for coffee with an array of traditional Christmas cookies called Plätzchen.

During the year, Rumtopf with ice cream would be served on special occasions as dessert. It used to last until well into summer. Nowadays, my mother and my younger brother keep up the tradition. In Goa the humid and hot climate does not support Rumtopf. I prepare a kind of Rumtopf-Ersatz whenever I feel like revisiting happy memories.

92 RUM RAISINS AND OTHER FRUITS IN ALCOHOL

I always have rum raisins in my fridge. Wash and clean the raisins, put them into a jar and douse them in rum.

INGREDIENTS

- 1 kg fruit

- ½ kg sugar
- Rum as needed

METHOD

Cover bottom of container with half a cup of sugar. Add fruit and sugar in layers and cover with alcohol. There should be a finger-wide of alcohol on top of fruit. Place container in a cool, dark place for one week. After this time, keep container in the fridge. Let fruit sit in alcohol for one month before serving.

A FRUITY AFFAIR

A decent Rumtopf-Ersatz works with fresh fruit. For this you need a ceramic or glass container that fits into your fridge. Most kinds of fruit work well with this method – strawberries, apples, cherries, pineapple, pears and grapes. I would not use bananas or papayas because they might turn into a mush.

LET'S EMBRACE LIFE

After more than fifty years on this planet, I can look into the mirror and tell myself: 'You do fine.' I try to live my life striving to behave like the best person I can be. I fail many times but this positive attitude has helped me take what life throws at me.

We all deal with problems, some more, some less. How we confront these problems, makes all the difference. For many years, I held a grudge against my parents – a really immature way to compensate for personal shortcomings. If you have read your way through this book, you know that I have struggled with emotional balance. I was pretty screwed up but in the end, I have come through. It is never too late to change; it is never too late to embrace life.

At this point, I would like to thank my parents. They have made me what I am and they have done what they could.

Let's be grateful for what we have, take a breath and say: life is beautiful.

PART 3

STRESS-FREE DINNER PARTIES

CHAPTER 9

ORGANIZATION IS KEY

Throwing a dinner party becomes an important skill when you grow older. Sharing food with family and friends remains one essential ingredient in a happy life. In my twenties, the main feature of a successful party was a stereo system with big speakers and plenty of drinks. When you mature, you tend to enjoy peaceful moments with friends and family gathered around the dinner table. Unfortunately, the host or hostess only gets to enjoy these parties if she has a well-trained staff or if she is well-organized.

The choice of dishes is of utmost importance when you throw a dinner party. I prefer recipes that I can prepare days in advance. You will find most recipes for the following dinner parties in this book but you need to adjust the amounts to the number of your guests. This will give you a fair idea for hosting great parties.

I start cooking one week before an event. I write down a shopping list and a time plan. Then I start preparing my dishes, relaxed and with ease. I believe your energy during cooking flows into the food and it influences the result. When I cook in a happy mood, my dishes taste better.

One of the most difficult things to gauge is the amount and kind of drinks needed. This depends on your habits and your friends. When I host a dinner party, I have a bar stocked with whiskey, vodka, gin, rum and some other goodies like coffee liqueur. I also keep limes on a chopping board together with a knife at the bar, so people can help themselves.

Many of our friends drink wine, but I never know if they prefer red or white wine. I buy at least one bottle of wine per guest. Then you need some soft drinks and juices. Buy tomato juice if somebody fancies a Bloody Mary. If your friends favour beer, buy plenty. Beer drinkers generally down quite a few bottles in the course of one evening.

For a dinner party, you need to be in control of three areas: the welcome space with a bar, the dinner table and the kitchen. You need to know how many glasses, plates and cutlery you need. Think well in advance about playlists for music and about decoration.

It is important for a successful dinner party that you select a date that gives you enough time before the event. When I host a dinner, I try to keep the afternoon before the event free from any other obligations. You need at least one hour for yourself before the guests arrive. Your work in the kitchen should be finished at this point and you should get ready. Here are some dinner plans to give you an idea of effortlessly hosting people at home.

1 DINNER PARTY WITH CHICKEN

MENU

- ♥ Welcome drinks, nuts/olives
- ♥ Chicken liver pâté, onion jam and garlic bread
- ♥ Chicken–pesto rolls, oven-roasted potatoes, mixed salad
- ♥ Chocolate–walnut cake with vanilla ice cream

SHOPPING LIST

(Serves 8)

In the pantry:
Brandy, garlic, sugar, salt, pepper, butter, extra virgin olive oil, coconut oil, red wine vinegar, white wine, flour, onions, beef or chicken stock, raw sugar, icing sugar, baking powder, wooden toothpicks, vanilla essence

Chicken liver pâté:
500 gm chicken liver, 500 gm salted butter, fresh thyme

Onion jam:
1 kg onions

Garlic bread:
2 baguettes, 500 gm salted butter, 2 bunches parsley, preferably flat leaf parsley

Chicken-pesto rolls:
8 boneless chicken breasts (one chicken has 2 breasts), 10 tbsp pesto

Oven-roasted potatoes:
1.5 kg potatoes, fresh or dried rosemary

Mixed salad:
Green salad leaves, cherry or normal tomatoes, 2 red or yellow peppers, fresh basil, rucola

Chocolate–walnut cake:
6 eggs, cacao powder, 200 gm walnuts, vanilla ice cream

TIME PLAN

1 WEEK (OR LONGER) BEFORE

Prepare the chicken liver pâté, onion jam and garlic butter.

You can freeze the required amount of chicken liver pâté, onion jam and garlic butter. That means you can prepare these up to two months in advance. The pâté keeps well for one week in the fridge. Onion jam and garlic butter can be kept in the fridge for two weeks easily.

Order the required amount of chicken breasts, baguette for the garlic bread, vanilla ice cream and salad to be picked up the day before the dinner party.

Make a list of drinks required for your party. Think about ice cubes. Do you need to buy some or can you make enough in your freezer? Check your glasses, cutlery, plates, table linen and napkins. You require a set of small plates for the starters, a set of big plates for the main course and a set of small plates for the cake. If you have to buy anything, do it now. Remember that you need an extra set of glasses for welcome drinks.

2 DAYS BEFORE

Prepare the chocolate cake and keep it in the fridge. Buy the drinks.

1 DAY BEFORE

Buy the chicken, baguette, vanilla ice cream, salad and, if needed, ice cubes and paper napkins. Buy some nuts and/or olives to serve with welcome drinks.

Prepare the chicken-pesto rolls. Do not coat them with flour; just secure them with toothpicks. Keep them in a sealed container in the fridge.

Place white wine, champagne and soft drinks in the fridge. If you don't have enough fridge space, do it on the day of the party. Remove all the food you will serve five hours before the party and cool the drinks. Or make an improvised fridge with a big container filled with ice blocks from an ice factory or store-bought ice cubes.

THE DAY OF THE PARTY

In the morning:
If you have frozen chicken liver pâté, onion jam and/or garlic butter, take it out from the freezer to defrost.

In the afternoon:
Prepare the roasted potatoes and keep them covered. Clean the salad and keep it ready in a big bowl. Prepare the vinaigrette and keep it in a glass with a tight-fitting lid. Fry the chicken-pesto rolls and keep them covered in the pan. For eight people you need to prepare two big pans. Keep the meat in one pan when it is fried and use the other pan to make the sauce.

Prepare the garlic bread and keep it on cookie sheets or stainless steel plates. Place the pâté and the onion jam into bowls ready for serving. Prepare dishes and spoons to serve the chicken-pesto rolls and the roasted potatoes. Keep the plates for the dessert in the kitchen.

Take out the cake from the fridge. If you want, you can also serve it chilled.

Set up your dinner table with table linen, napkins, cutlery, plates and glasses. Prepare an extra set of glasses for welcome drinks. Remember to keep big spoons to serve the dishes.

Place olives and/or nuts into bowls ready to be served. Keep napkins handy with the welcome drinks. Remember to have ice cubes and lemons at hand for the welcome drinks.

One hour before the party starts:
Stop the work and get ready.

When the guests arrive:
Have one or two welcome drinks and enjoy.

Ten minutes before you want to serve the dinner:
Warm up the garlic bread in the oven at lowest temperature.

When the garlic bread is warm, place the roasted potatoes in the oven, call everybody to the table and serve the starters.

When your guests have finished with the starters, ask somebody to collect the plates and bring them into the kitchen. While this is being done, heat up the chicken-pesto rolls. Mix the vinaigrette, pour it over the salad and mix it. Place the hot roasted potatoes and the chicken-pesto rolls in the serving dishes and serve the main dish.

When your guests have finished eating, collect all the dishes. Slice the cake. Place one slice of cake on each plate and add one spoonful of ice cream. It helps a lot to use an ice cream scoop for this job.

Serve the dessert. If you feel up to it, offer coffee or tea at this point.

2 DINNER PARTY WITH SEAFOOD

MENU

- Welcome drinks, nuts/olives
- Tuna pâté, mixed salad, garlic bread
- Fish soup
- Apple crumble with vanilla ice cream

SHOPPING LIST

(Serves 8)

In the pantry:
Garlic, sugar, salt, pepper, peppercorns, bay leaves, butter, extra virgin olive oil, coconut oil, red wine vinegar, flour,

onions, sugar, brown sugar, vanilla essence, cinnamon powder, clove powder, rum raisins, rolled oats

Tuna pâté:
1 tin tuna in oil (about 250 gm fish), 250 gm butter

Mixed salad:
Green salad leaves, cherry or normal tomatoes, 2 red or yellow peppers, fresh basil, rucola

Garlic bread:
2 baguettes, 500 gm salted butter, 2 bunches parsley (preferably flat-leaf parsley)

Fish soup:
Bones and head of a fish around 1.5 kg heavy, 1 kg red tomatoes, 1 tin (400 gm) peeled Italian tomatoes, 3 stalks celery, ½ kg onions, 4 big carrots, 1 bundle parsley, plenty of bread of your choice to mop up the soup, for example, 3 baguettes

Fresh seafood for the soup:
1 kg fish fillet, 1 kg cleaned prawns, 1 kg squids, 1 kg mussels (optional)

Apple crumble:
1.5 kg apples, 2 lemons or lime, desiccated coconut flakes

TIME PLAN

1 WEEK (OR LONGER) BEFORE

Prepare the tuna pâté and garlic butter.

You can freeze the required amount of pâté and garlic butter. That means you can prepare these up to two months in advance. The pâté keeps well for one week in the fridge. Garlic butter can be kept in the fridge for two weeks easily.

Order the required amount of baguette for the garlic bread, vanilla ice cream and salad, to be picked up the day before the dinner party. Place the order for the seafood that goes into the fish soup. You have to buy it on the day of the party. Order the fish for the fish stock. You can make the fish stock well in advance.

Make a list of drinks required for your party. Think about ice cubes. Do you need to buy some or can you make enough in your freezer? Check your glasses, cutlery, plates, table linen and napkins. You require a set of small plates for the starters, a set of big plates for the main course and a set of small plates for the dessert. Don't forget a big vessel for the fish soup. If you have to buy anything, do it now. Remember that you need an extra set of glasses for welcome drinks.

4 DAYS BEFORE

Prepare the fish stock for the fish soup and keep it in the fridge.

2 DAYS BEFORE

Prepare the apple crumble and keep it in the fridge.

1 DAY BEFORE

Buy the baguette, the vanilla ice cream, salad and, if needed, ice cubes and paper napkins. Buy some nuts and/or olives to serve with welcome drinks.

Place white wine, champagne and soft drinks in the fridge. If you don't have enough fridge space, do it on the day of the party. Remove all the food you will serve five hours before the party and cool the drinks. Or make an improvised fridge with a big container filled with ice blocks from an ice factory or store-bought ice cubes.

THE DAY OF THE PARTY

In the morning:

If you have frozen tuna pâté and/or garlic butter, take it out from the freezer to defrost. Buy the seafood for the soup. Clean the seafood. Check the prawns for veins. Cut the squids and boil them in a pressure cooker for forty-five minutes. Wash the fish fillets and cut them into bite-size pieces. If you cook mussels also, scrub the shells with a hard brush and remove the beards. Keep the seafood in the fridge.

In the afternoon:

Prepare the garlic bread and keep it on cookie sheets or stainless steel plates. Place the pâté and the onion jam into bowls ready for serving.

Clean the salad and keep it ready in a big bowl. Prepare the vinaigrette and keep it in a glass with a tight-fitting lid.

Prepare the fish soup. Fry the mussels in a pan and keep the opened ones. Slice the bread and place it into a basket or on a big platter, ready to be served.

Take out the cake from the fridge. If you want, you can also serve it chilled.

Set up your dinner table with table linen, napkins, cutlery, plates and glasses. Prepare an extra set of glasses for welcome drinks. Remember to prepare a big ladle for the fish soup and spoons for the salad and the other dishes.

Place olives and/or nuts into bowls so they are ready to be served. Keep napkins handy with the welcome drinks. Remember to have ice cubes and lemons at hand for the welcome drinks.

One hour before the party starts:
Stop the work and get ready.

When the guests arrive:
Have one or two welcome drinks and enjoy.

Fifteen minutes before you want to serve the dinner:
Warm up the garlic bread in the oven at lowest temperature.

Bring the fish soup to a boil. Add the fish fillets and let them simmer for five minutes. Add the opened mussels and the squids and let them simmer for two minutes. Add the prawns and switch off the fire. The soup should be hot enough to cook the prawns and stay warm until your guests have finished the first course.

When the garlic bread is warm, shake the vinaigrette and mix it with the salad. Call everybody to the table and serve the starters.

When your guests have finished with the starters, collect the plates and bring them into the kitchen. Ask somebody to take the bread to the table. Carefully fill the soup into your serving vessel and take it to the table.

When your guests have finished eating, collect all the dishes.

Place a helping of apple crumble onto each dessert plate and add one spoonful of ice cream. It helps a lot to use an ice cream scoop for this job.

Serve the dessert. If you feel up to it, offer coffee or tea at this point.

3 VEGETARIAN DINNER PARTY

MENU

- Welcome drinks, nuts/olives
- Hummus, mixed salad, garlic bread
- Vegetarian lasagne
- Fruit salad with vanilla ice cream

SHOPPING LIST

(Serves 8)

In the pantry:
Garlic, icing sugar, salt, pepper, butter, extra virgin olive oil,

red wine vinegar, onions, sugar, brown sugar, homemade vanilla essence

Hummus:
Chickpeas, tahini, lemons

Mixed salad:
Green salad leaves, cherry or normal tomatoes, 2 red or yellow peppers, fresh basil, rucola

Garlic bread:
2 baguettes, 500 gm salted butter, 2 bunches parsley (preferably flat-leaf parsley)

Vegetarian lasagne:
Lasagne sheets (best is Italian with non-cook printed on the packet), 1 litre milk, 600 gm mozzarella cheese, 2 packets tomato puree, 3 onions, 1 carrot, 400 gm white button mushrooms

Fruit salad:
2 kg fruits, 200 gm walnuts or any other kind of nuts, 6 lemons

TIME PLAN

1 WEEK (OR LONGER) BEFORE

Prepare hummus and garlic butter.

You can freeze the required amount of hummus and

garlic butter. That means you can prepare hummus up to two months in advance. Hummus keeps well for up to four days in the fridge. Garlic butter can be kept in the fridge for two weeks easily.

Order the required amount of baguette for the garlic bread, vanilla ice cream, mushrooms and salad, to be picked up the day before the dinner party. Buy the lasagne sheets also because sometimes they are difficult to find.

Make a list of drinks required for your party. Think about ice cubes. Do you need to buy some or can you make enough in your freezer? Check your glasses, cutlery, plates, table linen and napkins. You require a set of small plates for the starters, a set of big plates for the main course and a set of small plates for the dessert. If you have to buy anything, do it now. Remember that you need an extra set of glasses for welcome drinks.

4 DAYS BEFORE

If you have not prepared and frozen your hummus yet, do it now.

2 DAYS BEFORE

Prepare the tomato sauce and keep it in the fridge.

1 DAY BEFORE

Buy the baguette, the vanilla ice cream, and salad and, if needed, ice cubes and paper napkins. Buy some nuts and/or olives to serve with welcome drinks.

Place white wine, champagne and soft drinks in the fridge. If you don't have enough fridge space, do it on the day of the party. Remove all the food you will serve five hours before the party and cool the drinks. Or make an improvised fridge with a big container filled with ice blocks from an ice factory or store-bought ice cubes.

THE DAY OF THE PARTY

In the morning:
If you have frozen hummus and/or garlic butter, take it out from the freezer to defrost.

In the afternoon:
Prepare the garlic bread and keep it on cookie sheets or stainless steel plates. Place the hummus into bowls ready for serving.

Clean the salad and keep it ready in a big bowl. Prepare the vinaigrette and keep it in a glass with a tight-fitting lid.

Prepare the lasagne. Grate the mozzarella cheese. Make the béchamel sauce. Butter the baking dish. Clean and slice the mushrooms. Assemble the lasagne and bake it in the oven until the cheese on top of the lasagne has browned a bit. Keep it covered.

Prepare the fruit salad. Chop the nuts. Keep the fruit salad in the fridge.

Set up your dinner table with table linen, napkins, cutlery, plates and glasses. Prepare an extra set of glasses for welcome drinks.

Place olives and/or nuts into bowls, ready to be served.

Keep napkins handy with the welcome drinks. Remember to have ice cubes at hand for the welcome drinks.

One hour before the party starts:
Stop the work and get ready.

When the guests arrive:
Have one or two welcome drinks and enjoy.

Fifteen minutes before you want to serve the dinner:
Warm up the garlic bread in the oven at lowest temperature.

When the garlic bread has warmed up, take it out and place the lasagne in the oven.

Shake the vinaigrette and mix it with the salad. Call everybody to the table and serve the starters.

When your guests have finished with the starters, collect the plates and bring them into the kitchen. Take the lasagne to the table and serve it. If you want, you can serve the mixed salad together with the lasagne instead of the hummus. But lasagne is a filling dish; I don't think you need anything together with it.

When your guests have finished eating, collect the dishes.

Mix the fruit salad with the chopped nuts, the vanilla essence/alcohol and the icing sugar. Place one or two balls of vanilla ice cream on the dessert plates and serve them. An ice cream scoop helps a lot with this job.

Bring the fruit salad to the dining table with a big spoon. I prefer that guests help themselves with the salad. You never know how much fruit they like. If you feel up to it, offer coffee or tea at this point.

A BIG THANK YOU

I have written this book to the best of my knowledge and experience. What is right for me might not be good for you. Trust your own judgement, especially when it comes to food. We are all different. The proverb from the 17th century: one man's meat is another man's poison, still applies.

Please never stick to any of my recipes. Feel free to experiment, to remodel my directions to your taste. You cannot fight about matters of taste. Remember, there is a lot of joy to be found by successful experimenting in the kitchen. I would be happy if I could have inspired you. Thank you, dear reader; you make a huge difference in my life.

MEASURING INGREDIENTS WITH TABLES

I love cooking by feeling. That means I don't like to fiddle with measuring or balancing ingredients. Using measuring cups, which you can buy in any home equipment store, is the easiest way to get amounts right. I use measuring cups with 200 millilitres. The standard measuring cup in the US is 240 or 250 millilitres.

If you don't want to use measuring cups for whatever reason, please check the following tables to calculate amounts.

MEASURING DRY INGREDIENTS

Metric	Cups
50 ml	¼ cup
100 ml	½ cup
150 ml	¾cup
200 ml	1 cup

Millilitres	Spoons
1.25 ml	¼ teaspoon (tsp)
2.5 ml	½ teaspoon
5 ml	1 teaspoon
15 ml	1 tablespoon (tbsp)

Metric	Imperial	Metric	Imperial
15 gm	½ oz	250 gm	8 oz
30 gm	1 oz	280 gm	9 oz
60 gm	2 oz	315 gm	10 oz
90 gm	3 oz	375 gm	12 oz
125 gm	4 oz	410 gm	13 oz
155 gm	5 oz	1 kg	2 lb
185 gm	6 oz	1.5 kg	3 lb
220 gm	7 oz		

Metric	Imperial
30 ml	1 fl oz
60 ml	2 fl oz
90 ml	3 fl oz
120 ml	4 fl oz
155 ml	5 fl oz
170 ml	5½ fl oz
185 ml	6 fl oz
220 ml	7 fl oz
240 ml	8 fl oz
470 ml	16 fl oz
600 ml	20 fl oz (1 pt)

Metric	Imperial
750 ml	1¼ pt
1 litre	1¾ pt
1.2 litres	2 pt

1 cup of sugar	200 gm	7 oz
1 cup of flour	150 gm	5 oz

BIBLIOGRAPHY

Stoll, Andrew L., *The Omega-3 Connection*, New York: Simon and Schuster, 2012

Calbom, Cherie, *The Coconut Diet*, Thorsons, 2004

Swaab, Dick, *Wir Sind Unser Gehirn (Wij Zijn Ons Brein)*, Amsterdam: Droemer/Knaur, 2001

Somer, Elizabeth, *Eat Your Way to Happiness*, Harlequin, 2009

Wurtman, Judith J. and Frusztajer, Nina T., *The Serotonin Power Diet*, New York: Rodale Books, 2009

Breuning, Loretta Graziano, *Meet Your Happy Chemicals*, Oakland: Createspace, 2012

Church, Matt, *Adrenaline Junkies & Serotonin Seekers*, Berkeley: Ulysses Press, 2004

Davidson, Richard and Begley, Sharon, *The Emotional Life of Your Brain*, London: Plume, 2012

Hedaya, J. Hedaya, *The Antidepressant Survival Guide*, New York: Harmony, 2001

Orbach, Susie, *Fat Is a Feminist Issue*, London: Arrow, 2006

Graham, Tyler and Ramsay, Drew, *The Happiness Diet*, New York: Rodale, 2011

Websites
http://abcnews.go.com/Health/story?id=4115033&page=1
http://altered-states.net/barry/newsletter260/
http://archpedi.jamanetwork.com/article.aspx?articleid=1173883
http://articles.mercola.com/sites/articles/archive/2001/03/31/butter.
    aspx
http://blog.healthkismet.com/synthetic-vitamins-supplements-not-
    good-for
http://candycrush-cheats.com/candy-crush-addiction-science/
http://chriskresser.com/why-fish-stomps-flax-as-a-source-of-
    omega-3
http://consciouslifenews.com/8-foods-naturally-increase-
    melatonin-better-sleep/
http://curiosity.discovery.com/question/how-do-comfort-foods-
    work
http://draxe.com/top-8-health-benefits-of-butter/
http://drbenkim.com/articles-vitamins.html
http://drpatontheback.blogspot.in/2012/02/nervous-endocrine-
    and-immune-system.html
http://ejmas.com/pt/ptart_shin_0400.htm
http://emedicine.medscape.com/article/125350-overview
http://EzineArticles.com/6303962
http://faculty.washington.edu/chudler/bbb.html
http://greatist.com/health/surprising-high-fiber-foods
http://healing.answers.com/physical-health/the-relation-between-
    sleep-and-serotonin
http://health.msn.co.nz/healthyeating/nutrition/8658111/eating-
    comfort-foods-can-aid-weight-loss
http://healthyeating.sfgate.com/importance-vitamins-body-5846.
    html#page2
http://healthysleep.med.harvard.edu/healthy/getting/overcoming/
    tips-top

http://healthysleep.med.harvard.edu/healthy/matters/benefits-of-sleep

http://io9.com/5925206/10-reasons-why-oxytocin-is-the-most-amazing-molecule-in-the-world/all

http://kidshealth.org/teen/your_mind/mental_health/cutting.html

http://lewisford.info/melatonin.html

http://life.gaiam.com/article/eat-boost-metabolism-and-all-day-energy-meal-planning-guide-recipes

http://lifestyle.inquirer.net/152456/for-a-better-mood-and-better-health-youve-got-to-feed-your-brain-too

http://magazine.good.is/articles/comfort-food-is-real-scientists-discover-good-mood-foods

http://magazine.good.is/articles/sleep-better-4-ways-to-manipulate-your-melatonin-levels-30daysofgood

http://neurosciencestuff.tumblr.com/post/38271759345/gut-instincts-the-secrets-of-your-second-brain

http://orthomolecular.org/resources/omns/v08n03.shtml

http://psychcentral.com/lib/about-oxytocin/0001386

http://psychology.about.com/od/biopsychology/p/NervousSystem.htm

http://psychology.about.com/od/findex/g/fight-or-flight-response.htm

http://psycnet.apa.org/psycinfo/2014-34446-001/

http://researchnews.osu.edu/archive/anxietycells.htm

http://science.howstuffworks.com/life/5-ways-your-brain-influences-your-emotions.htm#page=1

http://sciencereview.berkeley.edu/the-second-brain-the-science-of-the-gut-continues-to-make-good-on-its-promise-to-aid-in-the-understanding-and-treatment-of-mental-disorders-and-beyond/

http://serendip.brynmawr.edu/bb/kinser/Structure1.html

http://serendip.brynmawr.edu/bb/neuro/neuro99/web2/Benner.html

http://smah.uow.edu.au/medicine/mrc/history-omega3/index.html

http://whfoods.org/genpage.php?tname=nutrient&dbid=103

http://www.anandapaloalto.org/joy/BenefitsOfMeditation.html
http://www.angelfire.com/de/nestsite/micro17.html
http://www.antislavery.org/english/campaigns/cocoa_traders/
http://www.bbc.com/news/health-18779997
http://www.bbc.com/news/health-24625808
http://www.bodyandsoul.com.au/health/health+advice/10+benefit
    s+of+a+good+nights+sleep,17681
http://www.brainfacts.org/brain-basics/neuroanatomy/
    articles/2012/mapping-the-brain/
http://www.buzzle.com/articles/how-does-serotonin-affect-your-
    mood.html
http://www.care2.com/greenliving/7-little-known-benefits-of-
    sunlight.html
http://www.channel4.com/programmes/how-to-cook-like-heston
http://www.chemheritage.org/discover/media/magazine/articles/28-
    1-the-man-with-a-fish-on-his-back.aspx?page=1
http://www.chiro.org/nutrition/FULL/Marine_vs_Veggie_
    Omega-3.shtml
http://www.clevelandclinicwellness.com/mind/happiness/Pages/
    TheFood-MoodConnectionEatYourWaytoHappiness.aspx
http://www.dailymail.co.uk/health/article-2023511/Reaching-fatty-
    treats-really-DOES-make-happier-scientists-claim.html
http://www.davidlebovitz.com/
http://www.doctoroz.com/videos/dopamine-diet?page=3
http://www.doctorsresearch.com/articles4.html
http://www.drroyallee.com/
http://www.elsajonesnutrition.ie/index.php/good-mood-food/
http://www.ewg.org/2013sunscreen/the-trouble-with-sunscreen-
    chemicals/
http://www.fda.gov/AboutFDA/WhatWeDo/History/default.htm
http://www.fi.edu/learn/brain/exercise.html
http://www.fi.edu/learn/brain/stress.html
http://www.foodscience-avenue.com/2008/10/food-texture.html

http://www.harley.com/island-syndrome/24-hormones-and-neurotransmitters.html

http://www.healthline.com/health/depression/benefits-sunlight

http://www.healthline.com/human-body-maps/brain

http://www.heartfoundation.org.au/healthy-eating/fats/Pages/cholesterol.aspx

http://www.helpguide.org/life/sleep_tips.htm

http://www.helpguide.org/mental/types_of_antidepressants.htm

http://www.huffingtonpost.com/2013/04/19/adrenaline-cortisol-stress-hormones_n_3112800.html

http://www.invigorate360.com/reviews/essential-role-of-serotonin-for-improved-brain-function/

http://www.isodisnatura.ca/history_of_omega-3s.htm

http://www.jeffreyhollender.com/?p=208

http://www.livescience.com/35219-11-effects-of-oxytocin.html

http://www.livestrong.com/article/207432-adrenaline-cortisol/

http://www.mayoclinic.org/diseases-conditions/high-blood-cholesterol/in-depth/cholesterol/art-20045192

http://www.mayoclinic.org/healthy-living/stress-management/in-depth/stress/art-20046037

http://www.mcmanweb.com/dopamine.html

http://www.medicalnewstoday.com/articles/232248.php

http://www.medicalnewstoday.com/articles/249413.php

http://www.medicinenet.com/script/main/art.asp?articlekey=550

http://www.mindbodygreen.com/0-5999/10-Healing-Benefits-of-the-Sun.html

http://www.mnwelldir.org/docs/history/vitamins.htm

http://www.monsanto.com/products/Pages/monsanto-agricultural-seeds.aspx

http://www.monsanto.com/whoweare/Pages/default.aspx

http://www.naturalnews.com/016353_omega 3_fatty_acids_mental_health.html

http://www.naturalnews.com/036650_synthetic_vitamins_disease_

side_effects.htm

http://www.naturalnews.com/040537_brain_foods_dopamine_
production.html

http://www.ncbi.nlm.nih.gov/pmc/articles/PMC2972642/

http://www.ncbi.nlm.nih.gov/pubmed/12108819

http://www.ncbi.nlm.nih.gov/pubmed/23798048

http://www.nigella.com/

http://www.nlm.nih.gov/medlineplus/ency/article/002399.htm

http://www.nobelprize.org/nobel_prizes/themes/medicine/
carpenter/

http://www.nytimes.com/1983/09/27/science/domination-is-linked-
to-chemical-in-the-brain.html

http://www.nytimes.com/2012/04/22/magazine/how-exercise-
could-lead-to-a-better-brain.html?pagewanted=all

http://www.obesityaction.org/educational-resources/resource-
articles-2/nutrition/comfort-foods-why-do-they-make-us-happy

http://www.oxytocin.org/cuddle-hormone/

http://www.psmag.com/navigation/health-and-behavior/comfort-
food-myth-improve-mood-study-research-90564/

http://www.psychologytoday.com/blog/prefrontal-nudity/201111/
boosting-your-serotonin-activity

http://www.psychologytoday.com/blog/the-antidepressant-
diet/201008/serotonin-what-it-is-and-why-its-important-
weight-loss

http://www.psychologytoday.com/blog/two-takes-
depression/201104/comfort-foods-improve-moods

http://www.psychologytoday.com/blog/your-neurochemical-
self/201107/nature-gave-us-four-kinds-happiness

http://www.rd.com/slideshows/8-ways-to-naturally-increase-
endorphins/

http://www.sanescohealth.com/our-bodys-communication-system/

http://www.sci-news.com/genetics/science-oxytocin-receptor-gene-
face-recognition-01647.html

http://www.sciencemuseum.org.uk/broughttolife/techniques/
germtheory.aspx

http://www.scientificamerican.com/article/gut-second-brain/

http://www.scientificamerican.com/article/soil-depletion-and-
nutrition-loss/

http://www.slavefreechocolate.org/

http://www.spice-of-life.com/columns/melaton.html

http://www.telegraph.co.uk/foodanddrink/10604062/The-
importance-of-texture-in-food.html

http://www.thebodysoulconnection.com/EducationCenter/fight.
html

http://www.thedailysheeple.com/what-is-going-on-in-your-gut-
your-second-brain-bacteria-and-your-health_122013

http://www.thedoctorwithin.com/vitaminc/ascorbic-acid-is-not-
vitamin-c/

http://www.theguardian.com/lifeandstyle/wordofmouth/2013/
jul/02/food-texture-how-important

http://www.theguardian.com/science/2013/feb/03/dopamine-the-
unsexy-truth

http://www.thepositivemindblog.com/index.php/blog/thoughts_
or_feelings_which_comes_first

http://www.thesleepguru.co.uk/insomniatryptophan-melatonin-
and-serotonin/

http://www.thewellnessdoc.com/resources/vitamins/natural_
synthetic.asp

http://www.understand-andcure-anxietyattacks-panicattacks-
depression.com/brain-chemistry.html

http://www.utexas.edu/research/asrec/dopamine.html

http://www.vanderbilt.edu/AnS/psychology/health_psychology/
vitamins.htm

http://www.vitasouth.com/pages/Norepinephrine-Explained.html

http://www.webmd.com/depression/features/fish-oil-to-treat-
depression

http://www.webmd.com/depression/features/serotonin
http://www.westonaprice.org/nutrition-greats/royal-lee
http://www.whfoods.com/genpage.php?tname=george&dbid=75
http://www.wisegeek.com/what-is-the-connection-between-
    serotonin-and-dopamine.htm
http://www.yale.edu/agrarianstudies/colloqpapers/11coldam.pdf
http://www.yourhormones.info/hormones/oxytocin.aspx
https://faculty.washington.edu/chudler/nutr.html

ACKNOWLEDGEMENTS

Every book graces the light of day because many people have worked together for the sake of it.

My list of acknowledgements starts with Sathya Saran, who believed in my concept and saw it through. I would also like to thank Debasri Rakshit, Sunayna Saraswat and Rashi Mall Bhambri, the team at HarperCollins India, who did all the hard work involved to send the book to press.

Here in Goa, I would like to thank Margaret Mascarenhas for encouraging me and appreciating my cooking. Marianne Borgo has been invaluable with her enthusiasm and networking. Wendell Rodricks' cheerful appreciation of my recipes has contributed to my motivation.

Last but not least I am grateful to my family. I could not have written this book without my parents. May my late father rest in peace. My mother is always ready to send me recipes and share her experience.

My husband and son, used to being my personal guinea pigs, have shown patience while I concentrated long hours on the computer screen instead of cooking dinner. I would also like to thank Maria, my sister-in-law, for years of support.

I need to express my gratitude towards Frederick Noronha and Khalil Ahmed, my first publishers in Goa.

Finally, I would like to thank all the people who shared food with us over the years and all the people who bought my books. It has been, and is, a wonderful journey.